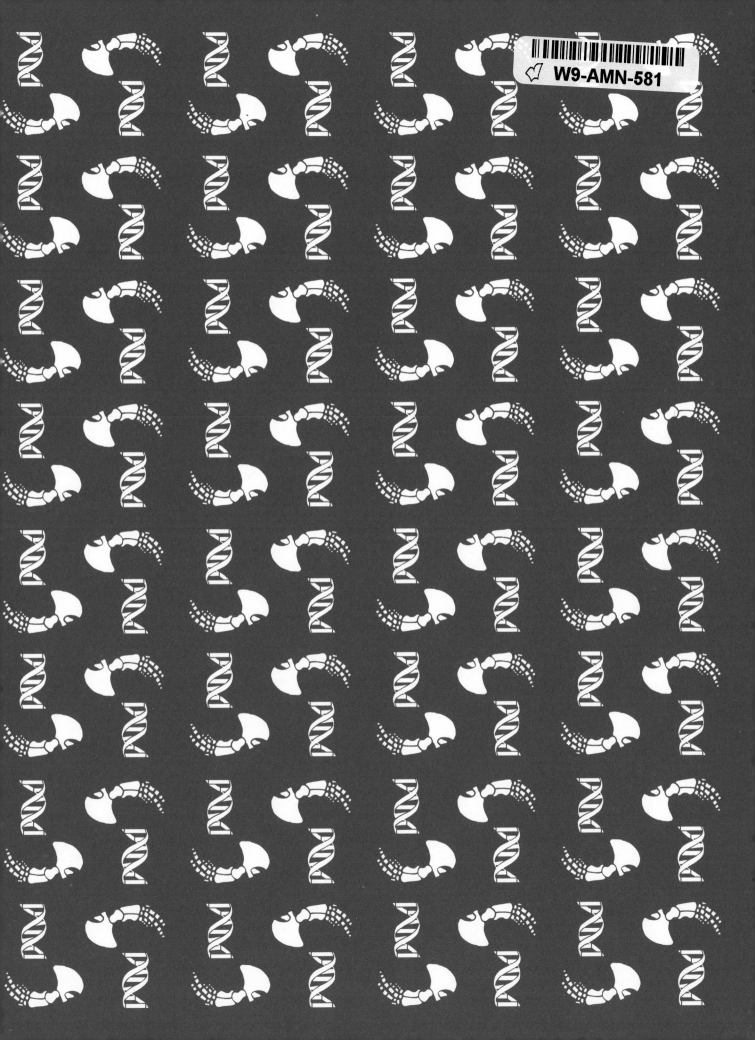

W9-AMN-581

EYEWITNESS ◉ SCIENCE

EVOLUTION

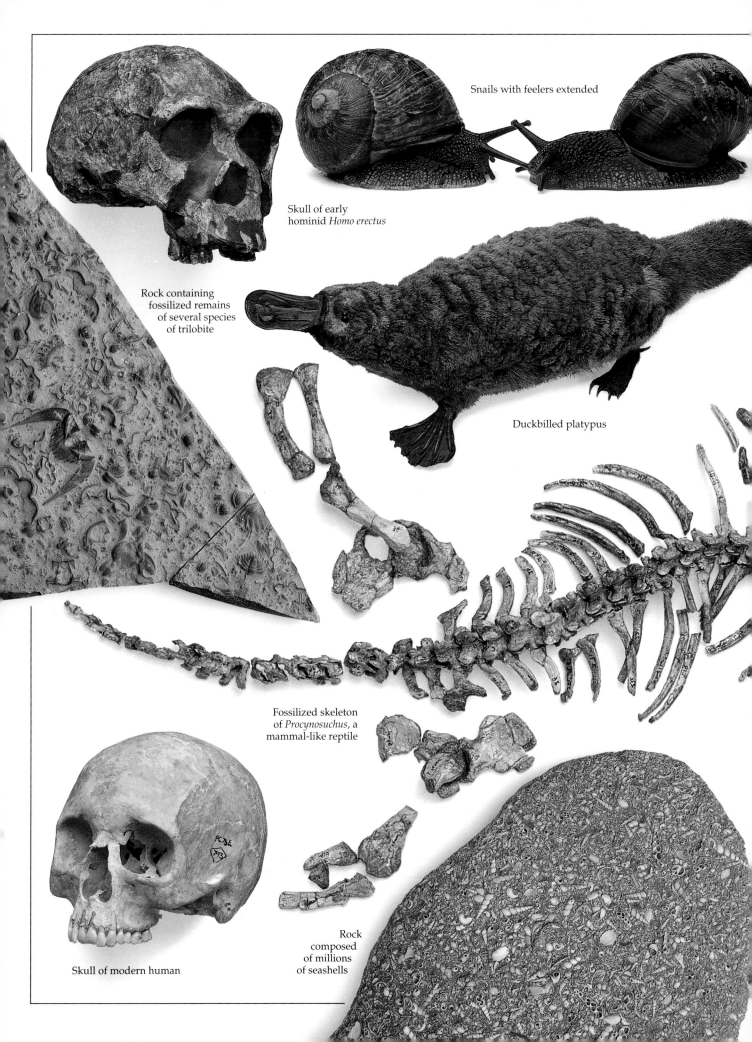

Snails with feelers extended

Skull of early
hominid *Homo erectus*

Rock containing
fossilized remains
of several species
of trilobite

Duckbilled platypus

Fossilized skeleton
of *Procynosuchus*, a
mammal-like reptile

Skull of modern human

Rock
composed
of millions
of seashells

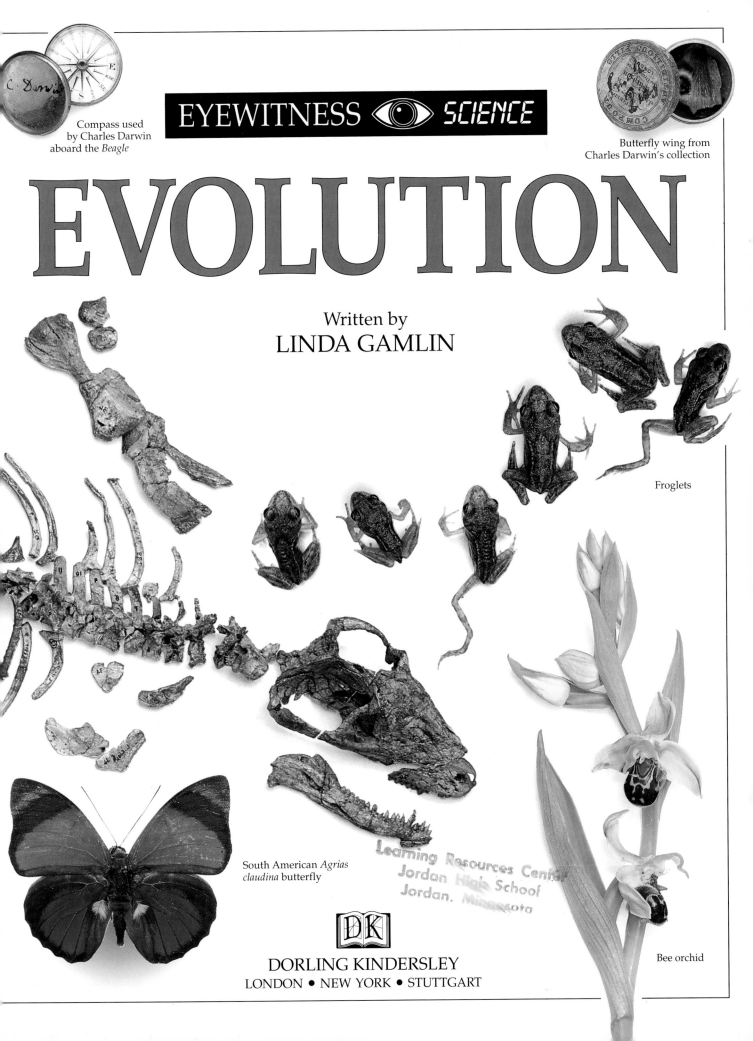

Compass used
by Charles Darwin
aboard the *Beagle*

EYEWITNESS SCIENCE

Butterfly wing from
Charles Darwin's collection

EVOLUTION

Written by
LINDA GAMLIN

Froglets

South American *Agrias
claudina* butterfly

Bee orchid

DK

DORLING KINDERSLEY
LONDON • NEW YORK • STUTTGART

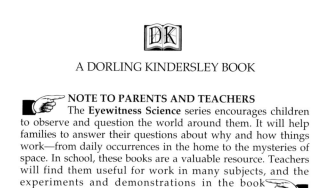

DK

A DORLING KINDERSLEY BOOK

NOTE TO PARENTS AND TEACHERS
The **Eyewitness Science** series encourages children to observe and question the world around them. It will help families to answer their questions about why and how things work—from daily occurrences in the home to the mysteries of space. In school, these books are a valuable resource. Teachers will find them useful for work in many subjects, and the experiments and demonstrations in the book can serve as an inspiration for classroom activities.

Project Editor Ian Whitelaw
Art Editor Jane Bull
Designer Marianna Papachrysanthou
Production Adrian Gathercole
Managing Editor Josephine Buchanan
Senior Art Editor Thomas Keenes
Picture Research Deborah Pownall, Catherine O'Rourke
Special Photography Andy Crawford, Neil Fletcher,
Steve Gorton, Dave King, Harry Taylor
Editorial Consultant Professor J. Maynard Smith,
University of Sussex, Brighton
US Editor Charles A. Wills
US Consultant Professor O. Roger Anderson,
Teachers College, Columbia University

First American Edition, 1993
2 4 6 8 10 9 7 5 3 1

Published in the United States by
Dorling Kindersley, Inc., 232 Madison Avenue
New York, New York 10016

Library of Congress Cataloging-in-Publication Data
Gamlin, Linda.
    Evolution / Linda Gamlin. — 1st American ed.
        p.   cm.   — (Eyewitness science)
    Includes index.
    Summary: Text about and photography of experiments, animals, plants, bones, and fossils reveal the ideas and discoveries that have changed our understanding of the natural world and how life began.
    ISBN 1-56458-233-7
    1. Evolution (Biology)—Juvenile literature.   [1. Evolution.]
I. Title.   II. Series.
QH367.1.G37   1993
575—dc20   92-54478
                                                        CIP
                                                         AC

Reproduced by Colourscan, Singapore
Printed in Singapore by Toppan Printing Co. (S) Pte Ltd

"Hand" and "finger" bones of horse's leg

19th-century microscope

Beetl

Bones of armadillo's forelimb

Bones of dolphin's flipper

Contents

Members of the insect order Hemiptera

Creation stories

WHERE DO PEOPLE COME FROM? How did the world begin? Where do plants and animals come from? People have been thinking about these questions for thousands of years, and there are many answers in the form of traditional stories. Some of these stories tell of one God who created the world and everything in it, including people. Other stories have many gods, each of whom made different things and then fought great battles for control of the world. Not all stories describe the world as having been created, however. Some tell of the world growing out of nothing, or out of chaos, without any creator. According to Buddhist beliefs, there was no beginning: instead, the Universe goes through endless cycles of being and nonbeing. The stories are all very different, but they often try to explain certain things about life. Some explain why people get ill and die, or why there is night and day. They may also explain some minor features of living things, such as why snakes have no legs. More importantly, the stories often give people rules or guidelines for their lives. They may say something about the different ways in which men and women should behave, or how people should treat the animals and plants around them. Some religious authorities regard these stories as valuable lessons on how people should live, rather than as factual accounts of how life on Earth actually began.

CREATORS OF THE WORLD
The Japanese creation story tells that in the beginning there were eight gods. When the youngest two, Izanagi and Izanami, stirred the ocean with a jeweled spear, falling drops of water formed an island. They came to live there, and Izanami gave birth to all the islands of Japan.

IN THE BEGINNING
These 16th-century illustrations show the Biblical creation story, which Christians and Jews share. There are two versions of the story, both in the first book of the Bible, Genesis. In the first version, shown here, man and woman are made simultaneously on the sixth day of creation. In the second version of the story, God creates the first man, Adam, before any other living thing. He then plants the Garden of Eden and makes all the animals. His final act is to create the first woman, Eve.

Egg

HATCHED FROM AN EGG
This carving of a bird-headed god holding an egg comes from Easter Island in the Pacific Ocean. Here, tradition says that the first people hatched from eggs laid by birds. On other Pacific islands, people were said to have hatched from turtles' eggs or from rocks.

MAKER OF HUMANKIND
Carved by the people of Rurutu Island in the Pacific, this statue of the god Tangaroa is covered with tiny people that he has created. The same god appears in myths from other Pacific islands, but in some of these he is just one god among many, and not the creator.

FROM THE FIRE
As well as the great creation stories, there have always been minor legends explaining the origins of plants and animals. In Europe, salamanders were said to be born from flames. Salamanders do hide among damp logs and may have been seen rushing out from the flames of log fires.

Illustration from the Middle Ages, showing a salamander rising from the flames

Humans cling to Tangaroa's body

EXPLAINING THE WORLD
The Biblical Genesis story explains, among other things, why snakes have no legs. God forbade Adam and Eve to eat from the tree of knowledge of good and evil, but a serpent tempted Eve to eat the fruit. As a punishment, the serpent was told: "Upon thy belly shalt thou go and dust shalt thou eat."

DEADLY SCREAM
In Europe, one minor legend concerned the mandrake plant, whose roots are sometimes human-shaped. The legend claimed that mandrake roots cried out when pulled from the ground, and this shriek would kill anyone who heard it. This pagan belief survived into Christian times.

CHANGING FORMS
Stalked barnacles are often seen attached to driftwood. In medieval times, they were said to grow on trees and then to turn into barnacle geese that flew away. Scientific study of the living world, from the 16th century on, cast doubts on such legends, and careful observation gradually took their place.

Medieval drawing of barnacle goose "tree"

Imaginative medieval woodcut of the mandrake plant

Stalked barnacles on driftwood

Fossils and fairytales

TAB.VII   chap:5.
1

ʄ.142.

Fossils are the remains or impressions of living things hardened in rock. People have been finding fossils for at least 30,000 years. Ice Age hunters made them into necklaces, and the idea that fossils had magical properties may well have begun then. Magical beliefs about fossils became common all over the world. The Chinese kept tiny fossilized fish in their food stores to keep away insect pests called silverfish. The Roman scholar Pliny the Elder wrote that fossilized sea urchins could cure snake bites and ensure success in battle. He also collected some extraordinary "tall tales" to explain the origins of fossils: sea urchin fossils were said to be formed from balls of foam created by masses of entwined snakes. Other people developed theories to explain fossils in general. One idea was that the rain picked up the seeds and eggs of living things from the sea. When the rain fell and seeped into rocks, the seeds and eggs grew into stony replicas of their true selves. This was an attempt to explain why so many fossils are clearly sea creatures.

ELFIN FARE
Thinking they were fairy loaves, people in southern England kept fossil heart urchins like this in their pantries to ensure that there would always be bread for the family.

Dr. Plot's horselike illustration of the fossil

Fossil mold

STONE HORSES
This unusual fossil is the cast, or mold, of the inside of a shell called *Myophorella*. The shell itself has rotted away. The living animal was similar to an oyster, having two shells held together by a strong muscle. This left a circular mark on each side, and Dr. Robert Plot (1640-1696) interpreted these as eyes. With great imagination, he also saw two ears and a mane and declared that this was an attempt by the Earth's *vis plastica* to make a horse's head.

A more fanciful theory, popular from medieval times until the 17th century, was that the Earth had its own "creative force," or *vis plastica*, and this force was trying to make copies of living things.

Opening in skull for trunk

ONE-EYED MAN
When skulls like this were found in fossil form on the Mediterranean island of Sicily, the ancient Greeks imagined giant men, each with a single eye in his forehead. This belief gave rise to the legend of the one-eyed Cyclops. In fact, this is the skull of an elephant, and the hole is where its blood vessels and airways ran down to the trunk.

BLINDING THE GIANT
On a vase from ancient Greece, the hero Odysseus is shown blinding the Cyclops Polyphemus with an iron brand as he sleeps in his cave on Mount Aetna in Sicily. Odysseus and his companions were able to escape from the island but made an enemy of Poseidon the sea god, the father of the Cyclops.

Pliny the Elder believed that these fossils were stone tongues that fell to Earth during eclipses of the moon. In 1667, Niels Stensen found a dead shark and realized that they were simply sharks' teeth. He was not the first with a sensible explanation for fossils, but most people preferred the tall stories.

Root

Cutting edge

Fossilized sharks's teeth

MYTHICAL MONSTERS

During the last ice age 40,000 years ago, there were giant bears in Europe. Some died in caves while hibernating. Many were fossilized, because a landslide in a cave can quickly bury the body before the bones decompose. When the skulls of these bears, with their huge canine teeth, were found in the Middle Ages, they were thought to belong to fire-breathing "dragons."

Cave bear skull

Drawing of ammonite

SERPENTS OF STONE

In northern England the coiled fossils of ancient ammonites, sea animals like the living *Nautilus*, were once thought to be snakes that had been turned to stone by a saint. Local people even carved heads on to these "snake stones," just to prove the point.

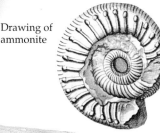

Grinding teeth

Canine tooth

Carved snake's head

Mythical winged dragon

FOSSIL FUNGUS?

Despite its toadstool-like appearance, this strange object is actually a sponge from an ancient sea. The sponge has become fossilized in flint. Toadstools themselves are far too soft ever to become fossilized.

Fossil ammonite

Victims of the flood

ONE OF THE GREATEST PUZZLES about fossils was the appearance of shells and other sea creatures high up on mountaintops. Some Ancient Greek scholars, such as Pythagoras and Herodotus, reasoned that such mountain rocks must once have been under the sea, but the early Christian philosopher Tertullian (c. AD 155-222) claimed that the waters of the flood, as described in the Bible, had carried shells up to this height. This idea was considered by Leonardo da Vinci (1452-1519), who made careful observations of fossils and calculated what would happen during a massive flood. He concluded that this explanation made no sense. Despite Leonardo's efforts, the idea remained popular among geologists until the late 18th century. By then the theory was known as diluvialism. It proposed that all the Earth's sedimentary rocks (rocks that are made up of layers of sand or silt) had been deposited during the 40 days of the flood, with all fossils being formed at the same time. As a popular notion, rather than a scientific theory, this survived into the 19th century, but by 1840 the evidence against it was so strong that the idea had largely disappeared.

NOAH AND THE FLOOD
The Bible describes an immense flood that covered all the Earth's land and lasted for 40 days. Noah had been told by God to build an ark and take on board a male and a female of every kind of animal, so that none of them would die out completely. This part of the story led to great debates when the fossils of large extinct animals were discovered (pp. 14-15).

Shelly rock from the top of Mount Snowdon in Wales

FOSSIL HUNTER
Johann Scheuzer (1672-1733), a Swiss fossil collector, was an enthusiastic "diluvialist" – one who believed that the flood had created all sedimentary rocks and fossils. He described one of his finds as "the bony skeleton of one of those infamous men whose sins brought upon the world the dire misfortune of the deluge." It was a fossil of a giant salamander.

RAISING THE ROCKS
During the 18th and 19th centuries, geologists began to understand how seashells could appear on mountain tops. They realized that most sedimentary rocks had been gradually formed under the sea by silt and sand. Here the fossils had formed when animals became buried by the sediment. Later on, movements of the Earth's crust squeezed some rocks and make them buckle upward, so that rocks that had been under the sea became the tops of mountains.

The missing fossils

If all fossils were creatures killed by the flood, there would be fossils of a great many land animals that drowned as the waters rose, but few fossils of fish, since they could swim. In fact, the opposite is true. Sea and river creatures are the most common fossils, while land animals are rare. It is now known that fossils cannot be formed easily on land, except in unusual places such as caves.

Rare fossil of an insect

Uncommon dragonfly fossil

Lizard

RARELY FOSSILIZED
While fossils of sea creatures such as brittle stars and fish are often found, fossils of land animals such as lizards and insects are rare.

SHELLY ROCK
Some rocks are made entirely of shells. Like coal and chalk, these could only have built up very slowly.

Fossilized brittle star, a marine animal

Chalk and coal

As people learned more about sedimentary rocks, it became clear that these could not have been laid down in 40 days. Chalk and coal, for example, are made up of the remains of living things – trillions of microscopic shells, in the case of chalk, and thousands of trees piled one upon another, in the case of coal. Clearly, such rocks must have taken a very long time to build up.

ROCK OF AGES
In 1858 a geologist, looking at chalk under the microscope, found that it was almost entirely made up of tiny shells. These shells belonged to microscopic creatures that floated at the ocean's surface. We know this because their relatives still do so today. Chalk cliffs (above) show how thick the layers of chalk are.

MICROSCOPIC STRUCTURE
This modern photograph of the structure of chalk was taken with a scanning electron microscope. It shows tiny circular platelets, parts of the minute creatures that make up the chalk.

Fossil perch

Fern fossil in coal

THE COAL FORESTS
Coal is made almost entirely of trees and other plants from swampy forests. When the trees fell into the water they did not rot away but gradually formed peat. This was then compressed by the growing weight above it, turning it into coal. Coal seams can be 66 ft (20 m) thick.

Jean Baptiste de Lamarck

JEAN BAPTISTE DE LAMARCK (1744-1829) was one of the first people to propose a theory of evolution. He believed that there were two evolutionary forces at work. The first was a "tendency to progression," an automatic process by which all living things became more complex. The second force was the need to fit in with the local environment: as animals tried to fit in, their efforts produced a bodily change. In this way the giraffe developed a long neck by stretching for the leaves of trees, and wading birds grew long legs by straining upward to keep themselves dry. These two forces were not in harmony, according to Lamarck. The first force working alone would produce perfect patterns of increasing complexity among animals, but the second force interfered with the first. For the second force to work, characteristics acquired by the parents (such as a longer neck) would have to be passed on to their offspring. This is now known not to happen, except in a few rare cases, but in Lamarck's day it was a common idea. For a century afterwards, many people, including Darwin (p. 20), believed it to be true. Today, the term "Lamarckism" is often used just to mean the inheritance of acquired characteristics. The other parts of Lamarck's theory have largely been forgotten.

HIGH AND DRY
According to Lamarck's theory, by trying to keep its belly out of the water a wading bird "acquires the habit of stretching and elongating its legs." In this way, he believed, species such as this purple heron developed their long legs.

Subtle fluids

Lamarck suggested that there were "subtle fluids" flowing all around a body and all through it, and that these produced both movement and change. He regarded the fluids as mysterious, but believed he could identify two: caloric (heat) and electricity.

CHARGED IDEAS
Lamarck believed that his "subtle fluids" were involved in both kinds of change – the "tendency to progression" and the striving to fit local conditions. Electricity was of great interest to scientists at the time, and it appealed to Lamarck because it could be felt but not seen. The French scientist Jean Antoine Nollet (1700-1770) set up experiments (right) to study the effects of static electricity on plants and animals.

FEELING THE WAY FORWARD
Lamarck used snails as an example of how "subtle fluids" worked. Snails have poor vision, and he imagined an ancestral snail with no feelers, groping around with its head. Its efforts to feel the way would send "masses of nervous fluid as well as other liquids" to the front of the head. In time this would produce feelers.

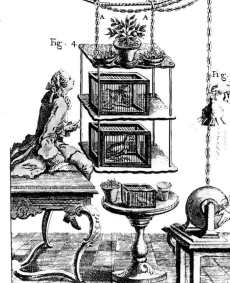

Extended feelers

Looking at the evidence

To support his claim that evolution had occurred, Lamarck pointed to the way that members of a species, such as a butterfly species, can vary from place to place. His ideas about the inheritance of acquired characteristics and about the continuous creation of simple life forms were later proven to be false.

Agrias claudina claudina
Eastern Central Brazil

Agrias claudina sardanapalus
Peru and Brazil

Agrias claudina claudianus
Southeastern Brazil

Agrias claudina lugens
Peru

SPONTANEOUS LIFE
If all living things are progressing, why are there still simple creatures left? Lamarck believed that new ones arose by "spontaneous generation" of microscopic life from nonliving matter, such as wet straw. French microbiologist Louis Pasteur (1822-1895) showed this to be an illusion. If the straw was boiled thoroughly, no living things developed.

PASSING IT ON
If acquired characteristics were inherited, as Lamarck thought, then the children of white-skinned people living in hot countries would be born with sun-tanned skins. This English family in 19th-century India shows that they are not.

MAKING NEW SPECIES
These lovely butterflies from different areas of South America illustrate Lamarck's point about variation within a species. Those from different areas can all interbreed, so they must all belong to the same species. They are called "subspecies." Lamarck also observed that closely related species (p. 22) can look very much alike, as similar as these subspecies. From this he concluded that related species had developed from a set of subspecies. This idea is now thought to be correct, although exactly how new species are formed is still being debated (p. 40).

Agrias claudina godmani
Central Brazil

Agrias claudina intermedius
Southeastern Colombia, Venezuela

POET AND BOTANIST
Even before Lamarck, the poet Johann von Goethe (1749-1832) had published evolutionary ideas about plants.

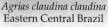

Extinct animals

ACCORDING TO THE BIBLE, Noah took two of every kind of animal into his ark, and all survived the Flood. Christianity also taught that each living thing was an essential link in God's chain of creation. Thus, it would be impossible for any of them to have died out completely, or become "extinct." When fossils of unknown creatures were found, it was assumed that the animals were still living somewhere in the world. However, by the end of the 18th century, the fossils of such gigantic creatures had been found that this explanation began to seem unlikely. In North America, the massive bones of the giant ground sloth and the mastodon were discovered. No unexplored regions were large enough to hide such giants, and the suspicion that they had become extinct began to grow. French scientists, less influenced by religious views following the upheavals of the French Revolution, were among the first to accept the idea of extinction. Afterwards, the idea was accepted in the US, and then, more slowly, in other countries.

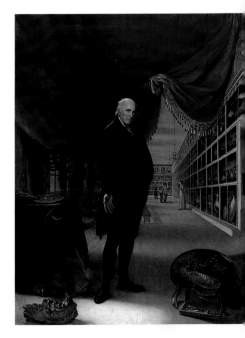

SCIENTIFIC PRESIDENT
Thomas Jefferson (1743-1826) was also a fossil collector. At first he could not accept that any animal had become extinct, but in time the evidence of the fossil finds convinced him that they had.

LOST WORLDS
The strange duck-billed platypus of Australia was only discovered by western science in 1799. Discoveries like this suggested that there were many unknown creatures in the world and that "extinct" animals could still be alive somewhere.

HARD TO HIDE
This is a cross-section, shown half life-size, through the upper molar teeth of a giant ground sloth, known as *Megatherium*. The fossils of another ground sloth, almost as large, were found in North America and first described by Thomas Jefferson in 1797. A living animal of this size clearly could not remain undiscovered, unlike small animals such as the platypus. By the 1830s the idea of extinction had become widely accepted.

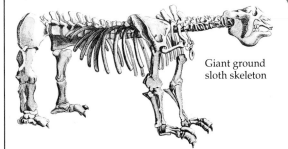

Giant ground sloth skeleton

PEALE'S MUSEUM (*left*)
Charles Willson Peale (1741-1827) was an artist, showman, and fossil collector. In 1799, together with Jefferson and others in the American Philosophical Society, he advertised for large fossil bones. In this way he was able to locate and excavate the skeletons of two mastodons, extinct relatives of the elephants. The bones were mounted to make a complete skeleton, and Peale displayed this in his museum of "natural curiosities."

Human second molar tooth

GIANT MOLAR
The second molar tooth of the mastodon, complete with its root, dwarfs a molar tooth from a human mouth. Giant mammals such as the mastodon were discovered before the first dinosaurs came to light. When the even larger remains of the dinosaurs were found, beginning in the 1820s (p. 18), the idea of extinction became widespread.

Second molar tooth of a mastodon

OUT OF THE PIT
Peale's mastodon skeleton was found in swampy ground, and the excavation was difficult. He had to design a machine to bale out the water from the pit. This was operated by a large treadwheel, and the tourists who flocked to see the excavation were put to work operating the wheel. Peale himself painted this dramatic picture of the scene. Americans became intensely proud of their extinct giants.

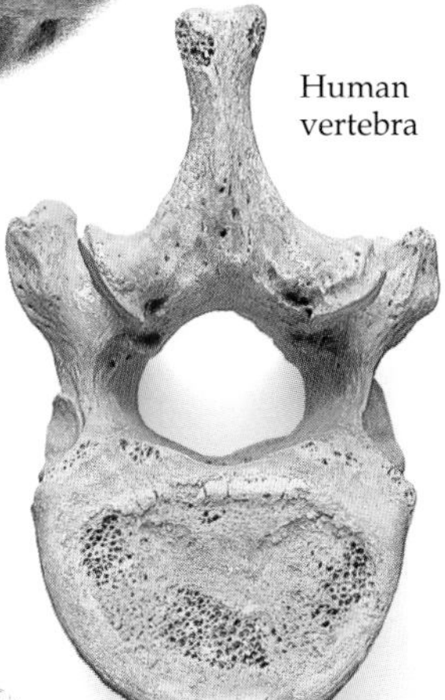

Human vertebra

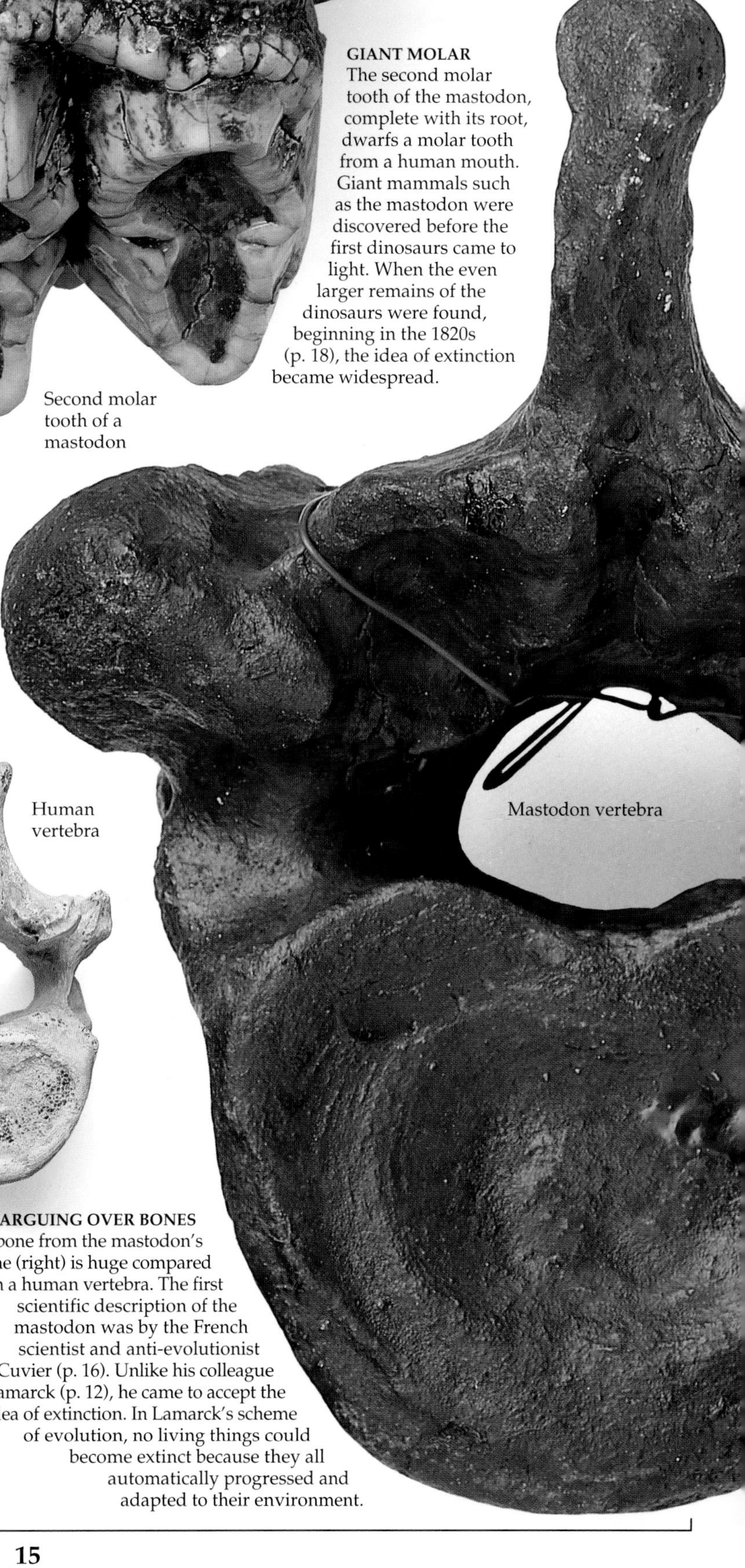

Mastodon vertebra

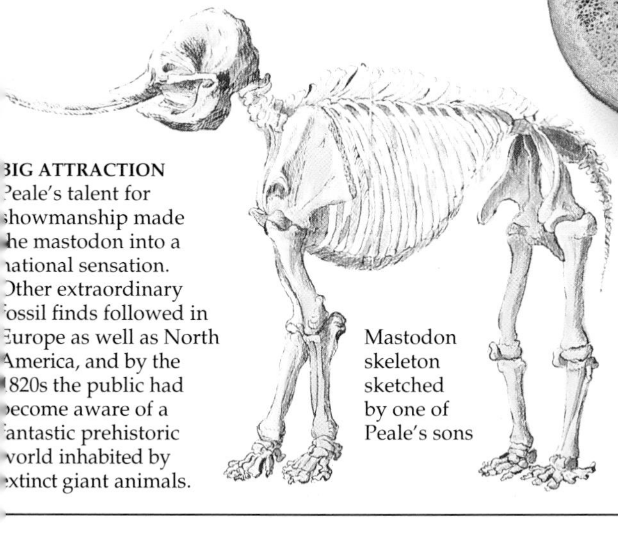

BIG ATTRACTION
Peale's talent for showmanship made the mastodon into a national sensation. Other extraordinary fossil finds followed in Europe as well as North America, and by the 1820s the public had become aware of a fantastic prehistoric world inhabited by extinct giant animals.

Mastodon skeleton sketched by one of Peale's sons

ARGUING OVER BONES
A bone from the mastodon's spine (right) is huge compared with a human vertebra. The first scientific description of the mastodon was by the French scientist and anti-evolutionist Cuvier (p. 16). Unlike his colleague Lamarck (p. 12), he came to accept the idea of extinction. In Lamarck's scheme of evolution, no living things could become extinct because they all automatically progressed and adapted to their environment.

A series of catastrophes

GEORGES CUVIER
Cuvier believed that catastrophes had stripped much of the Earth of life several times, but that some regions had always escaped, and animals had spread again from those regions. Later, he also accepted that some animals had become extinct, while Lamarck refused to believe this. Cuvier was against evolution, believing that life had "stood still" between catastrophes. Lamarck and Cuvier became lifelong enemies.

INDUSTRIAL EXPANSION in the 18th century created a need for iron ore and coal, as well as canals for transportation. Mines and excavations went deep into the Earth, which led to great advances in geology. By the early 19th century Abraham Werner (1750-1817) in Germany and William Smith (1769-1839) in the UK had established that rocks are made up of distinct layers called strata. These belonged to particular geological periods and eras, identified by the fossils found in them. Werner thought that there had been a series of catastrophic worldwide floods, each one laying down a layer of rock. It was the abrupt change in fossils from one geological era to another that led Werner and others to formulate these "catastrophe theories." Some identified each flood with a day of creation described in the Bible, but others realized that the rocks must have built up over thousands of years. Later catastrophists, including Frenchman Georges Cuvier (1769-1832), referred to earthquakes and climatic changes, as well as floods. The idea linking these theories was that the Earth had been shaped by unimaginably powerful forces, utterly different from those at work now. The opposite view, uniformitarianism, held that the Earth was built up gradually by everyday forces, such as erosion and deposition (p. 28).

EVIDENCE FROM EGYPT
Napoleon's troops invaded Egypt in 1798 and brought back mummies found in the pyramids. Among these was a mummified ibis, and Cuvier was jubilant to find that its skeleton was the same as that of a living ibis. He claimed this absence of change as evidence that Lamarck was wrong and that evolution did not occur.

UNCHANGED IBIS
The modern ibis is indeed the same as that of Ancient Egypt. Some species do stay much the same for thousands, or even millions, of years, while other species can evolve very rapidly. It all depends on the circumstances. Lamarck and Cuvier were each right on one point and wrong on another. Lamarck was right in thinking that species were not fixed, but Cuvier was partly right about mass extinctions (p. 46).

Egyptian sculpture of an ibis

Modern ibis

Mummified ibis

CLUES FROM CANALS

William Smith developed an interest in geology while constructing canals. He found that geological periods can be recognized by their fossils and that they always occur in the same order. Geologists today accept the uniformitarian view that most rock formations are due to gradual everyday forces, not catastrophes. The distinctions between geological eras are largely due to mass extinctions of living things (p. 46). They represent sudden biological changes, not geological ones.

Rock strata

Loam
Sand
Sandstone
Tilgate stone
Sandstone
Tilgate stone
Sandstone
White Rock near Hastings

William Smith

GEOLOGICAL MAP OF GLOUCESTERSHIRE by W.SMITH, Mineral Surveyor 1819

One of Smith's geological maps showing strata as different colors

Hugh Miller, Scottish stonemason and fossil hunter

MILLER'S FISH

Hugh Miller (1802-1856), a deeply religious man, found fossils of extinct armored fish. He believed, wrongly, that they were more advanced than living fish and saw them as part of an earlier creation destroyed by a catastrophe. Miller's books, which tried to reconcile geology with the Bible, were very popular.

Fossil fish found by Miller

Miller's paper model of extinct fish

CONTROVERSIAL FINDS

Miller helped to popularize a new religious version of catastrophe theory. It held that there had been several successive creations, each destroyed by a catastrophe, and that the Bible told only of the last creation. All fossils of extinct animals were from earlier creations. This theory was dealt a blow by finds from several British caves of extinct animals alongside handmade tools.

THE ICE MAN

American scientist Louis Agassiz (1807-1873), a follower of Cuvier, added a new type of catastrophe – the Ice Ages. Agassiz's theories were quickly rejected by many uniformitarians, such as Charles Lyell (1797-1875), who believed that all geological change was gradual. While modern geology has shown that Lyell's theory was closer to the truth than the catastrophe theories did, Agassiz's Ice Ages did occur. There were also many changes of sea level and of climate, but these were slow changes, not sudden catastrophes.

Mammoth tooth found with hand ax

Hand ax made by early people

17

Dinosaur frenzy

FOSSILIZED DINOSAUR BONES were discovered as early as the 17th century, but they were not recognized as belonging to giant reptiles. The breakthrough came with Gideon Mantell (1804-1892), a British doctor and fossil hunter. In 1822 he found some massive and unusual teeth which he showed to Cuvier (p. 16) and William Buckland, a British geologist. Both dismissed them as unimportant, but Mantell was convinced they were wrong and continued his research. Eventually, he found that the teeth resembled those of iguana lizards. Calling his find *Iguanodon* (iguana-tooth), he published a description of a lizard 40 ft (12 m) long. In the meantime, Buckland had found his own giant reptile. Such finds continued, but the name dinosaur ("terrible lizard") was not used until 1841, when it was coined by Richard Owen, a celebrated anatomist and follower of Cuvier. Dinosaurs created a sensation because they were so spectacularly different from anything still alive. They remained headline news throughout the 19th century, making everyone aware of the distant past and its strange animals. This awareness set the stage for evolutionary ideas. Yet Owen used the dinosaurs as an argument against evolution, since they were more advanced than living reptiles. Modern evolution theory recognizes that evolution does not always mean progress (p. 48). If the environment changes, more advanced animals may die out while their less advanced relatives survive.

DIGGING FOR *IGUANODON*
Excavations at the quarry in Sussex, southern England, from which Gideon Mantell's *Iguanodon* teeth originally came.

SURPRISING FINDS
William Buckland (1784-1856) displays some prize specimens. The long-beaked skull at the front is an *Ichthyosaur*, a marine reptile that belonged to a separate group from the dinosaurs. The first *Ichthyosaur* was described in 1810 but was thought to be a crocodile. In 1824 Buckland found jaw fragments and other bones of a dinosaur called *Megalosaurus*. Richard Owen supervised the making of a model *Megalosaurus* (below) in the 1850s, before any complete dinosaur skeletons had been found. With so little evidence Owen made a good guess, but the model is largely wrong. The same sculptor made the *Iguanodon* model opposite.

CONTROVERSIAL MODELS
This model of *Megalosaurus*, based on fossils found by Buckland, was later made into a life-size dinosaur and put on show at the Crystal Palace in London alongside others. When the civic leaders of New York commissioned a similar exhibition for Central Park, a local judge attacked the models as "anti-religious," and the scheme ended when someone broke into the workshop and destroyed all the models.

Jaw fragments found by Buckland

Fragments fitted into outline of skull

DARWIN'S ENEMY

Richard Owen (1804-1892), who coined the word "dinosaur," also wrote a scathing review of Darwin's *The Origin of Species* and predicted that Darwin would be forgotten in 10 years' time. In later life, Owen resented Darwin's fame and implied that he had developed an evolutionary theory of his own long before Darwin. Owen was present when, on New Year's Eve, 1853, 21 scientists ate dinner inside his model of the *Iguanodon* (below) before it joined other dinosaur models at London's Crystal Palace.

GIDEON MANTELL

On the basis of the bones and teeth that he had found, Mantell imagined *Iguanodon* to be like a large lizard. In his reconstruction Mantell placed the horn-like spike (below) on the tip of the animal's nose. It was later discovered to be a thumb spike.

DOZENS OF DINOSAURS

In 1878 coal miners in Belgium found 39 *Iguanodon* skeletons. Fossil footprints suggested that *Iguanodon* might have walked on its hind legs. It was believed to have stood semi-upright, so the skeletons of an emu and a wallaby were studied for this Belgian reconstruction.

Misplaced thumb spike

Cast of *Iguanodon* "horn"

HORN OF THE IGUANODON.
This extraordinary Fossil is described, Wonders of Geology,
Vol. I. p. 405.
THE ORIGINAL IN THE BRITISH MUSEUM.
J. TENNANT, GEOLOGIST, 149, STRAND, LONDON.

CHANGING IDEAS

This modern view of *Iguanodon* is based on detailed studies of marks on the bones, which can reveal much about muscles and tendons. They show that it walked mainly on two legs, with its horizontal body balanced by a rigid tail.

SECRET AUTHOR

In 1844, as dinosaur discoveries amazed the public, a pro-evolution pamphlet called *The Vestiges of Creation* was published. Robert Chambers (1802-1871) was revealed as its author only after his death. Chambers tried to make evolution respectable, but failed totally. Scientists did not take *Vestiges* seriously, as it was full of mistakes and innaccuracies.

SCALING UP

This model *Iguanodon* and other models were later scaled up to make the giant reptiles displayed at the Crystal Palace since 1854.

19

Charles Darwin

CHARLES DARWIN (1809-1882), THE ENGLISH NATURALIST, is well known as the author of *The Origin of Species*. He was not the first to think of evolution, and his real achievement was to make the idea respectable and collect a huge amount of evidence to show that evolution had occurred. In the early 19th century the concept of evolution was very unpopular. Lamarck's theory (p. 12) had been taken up in revolutionary France in the 1790s because it challenged the authority of the church and the king. The fear of a similar revolution in England made evolution a scandalous idea. Indeed, the zoologist Professor Robert Grant lost his position at the University of London and died in poverty because he openly supported Lamarck's views. When an anonymous pamphlet on evolution, *The Vestiges of Creation* (p. 19), was published in 1844, it met with outrage. All this encouraged Darwin to keep quiet for as long as possible." It is like confessing a murder," he wrote to a friend as his theory steadily took shape in his mind. In 1858, when the naturalist Alfred Wallace also hit upon the idea of natural selection (p. 36), Darwin was finally forced to publish.

Telescope used on the *Beagle*

Charles Darwin

TAKING NOTES
While living aboard the *Beagle*, Darwin took up the habit of making careful observations of the natural world. He also made long and detailed notes, recording everything that he saw, and he thought hard about the meaning of his scientific observations.

Darwin's compass

One of Darwin's notebooks

C. Darwin

HMS *Beagle*

From 1832 to 1836 Darwin was ship's naturalist on board the ship HMS *Beagle*, which sailed around the world. In South America, and particularly in the Galapagos Islands, he noted many puzzling features of the plants and animals that lived there. He later understood that these peculiarities were the results of evolution.

THINKING AFLOAT
Darwin was not an evolutionist when he stepped aboard the HMS *Beagle*, nor when he returned. But over the next five years the idea took shape in his mind. He was never dogmatic about his theory and considered all his opponents's views carefully. In later years this approach helped Darwin to gain support from some of the leading naturalists of his day – even those who had previously rejected evolution.

GOING ASHORE
On the voyage, Darwin took with him a copy of Charles Lyell's new book *Principles of Geology* in which Lyell claimed that the geological features of the Earth could be explained by slow-acting forces that were still at work, such as the laying down of sediment. Darwin spent much time ashore, and his observations of geology confirmed Lyell's theory, implying that the Earth was very old.

People of Tierra del Fuego greet the *Beagle*

Buenos Ayres (city) Beagle channel

A great naturalist

Before the *Beagle* voyage, Darwin studied to be a clergyman at Cambridge University. While there, he developed a passionate interest in natural history – an interest that was to change the course of his life.

ERASMUS DARWIN

Charles's grandfather, Erasmus Darwin (1731-1802), was a doctor, poet, and botanist. He was also a friend of scientists and industrialists, such as Joseph Priestley and Josiah Wedgwood, who questioned conventional ideas and were considered dangerous. Even before Lamarck (p. 12) he wrote books that contained evolutionary ideas. The next generation of the Darwin family, anxious to seem more respectable, largely ignored Erasmus's books.

Erasmus Darwin

Ivory handle

Scissors used in dissection

Magnifying glass

Lens

Mounted needle used in dissection

Butterfly wing

Part of Darwin's beetle collection

BEETLE MANIA

During his student days at Cambridge, Darwin was an enthusiastic collector of beetles. This is part of his enormous collection. Being an experienced practical naturalist was a great strength for Darwin. When it came to discussing plants and animals, he had first hand knowledge of the subject.

ALL ABOUT WORMS

After writing *The Origin of Species*, Darwin continued his work as a naturalist. He felt that looking at the small details of living things was just as important as devising grand theories. One of his later books was devoted entirely to earthworms, which clearly puzzled this cartoonist.

A cartoon from the humorous magazine *Punch*

COLLECTING DATA

Darwin grew many plants in the glasshouses at his home, Downe House. He was particularly interested in climbing and twining plants, insect-eating plants, and orchids. He dissected the flowers of orchids and made some amazing discoveries about how these flowers are pollinated. Other naturalists sent him seeds or whole plants that might interest him, and some of the seed packets have survived to this day (right). Darwin's work would have made him famous as a great biologist even if he had never written *The Origin of Species*.

Collecting boxes, beetle, and microscope slide from Downe House

Seed packet sent to Darwin

Seeds

From The Royal Gardens, KEW.

Living evidence

THINKING THE SAME WAY
Constantine Rafinesque was an eccentric American naturalist who saw the signs of evolution.

DARWIN SET HIMSELF two major tasks. One was to work out a mechanism by which evolution might occur. The mechanism he thought of was natural selection (p. 36), which is still accepted today as the main force behind evolution. His other task was to collect enough evidence to convince people that evolution had occurred. Some evidence came from fossils (p. 26) or from plant and animal distribution (p. 24). Equally important was the evidence from living things. This was clear enough to have been noticed by other naturalists, including Constantine Rafinesque, who wrote in 1836, "All species might have been varieties once, and many varieties are gradually becoming species." Such casual remarks by naturalists carried little weight, but Darwin was more difficult to ignore because he produced so much data. One important piece of evidence was that the same basic pattern of bones appears in the limbs of all mammals. Such similarities show that they must all be descended from a common ancestor.

CHIMPANZEE'S ARM
The arm and hand of the chimpanzee are close to the basic vertebrate pattern, having five fingers, five hand bones, a set of small bones in the wrist, two lower arm bones, and one upper arm bone. In these drawings the different bones are color-coded.

Finger bones

Hand bones

Wrist bones

Lower arm bones

Upper arm bone

Lower arm bones

Finger bones

Wrist bones

Chimpanzee's arm

BEE ORCHIDS
These Mediterranean bee orchids look remarkably similar, but they cannot interbreed. Therefore, each of them belongs to a separate species. Each species is pollinated by a different type of insect, and this acts as an isolating mechanism (p. 41). Darwin and Rafinesque were both struck by groups of very similar species such as these. It seemed obvious that they must have evolved from a single ancestral species. This ancestor probably developed into a number of varieties or subspecies (p. 13) first.

Bat

Bones of bat's wing

BAT'S WING
In bats, the hand and finger bones have developed into supports for the membranes of the wing. The similarity in basic structure between a bat's wing and a dolphin's flipper is strong evidence for evolution.

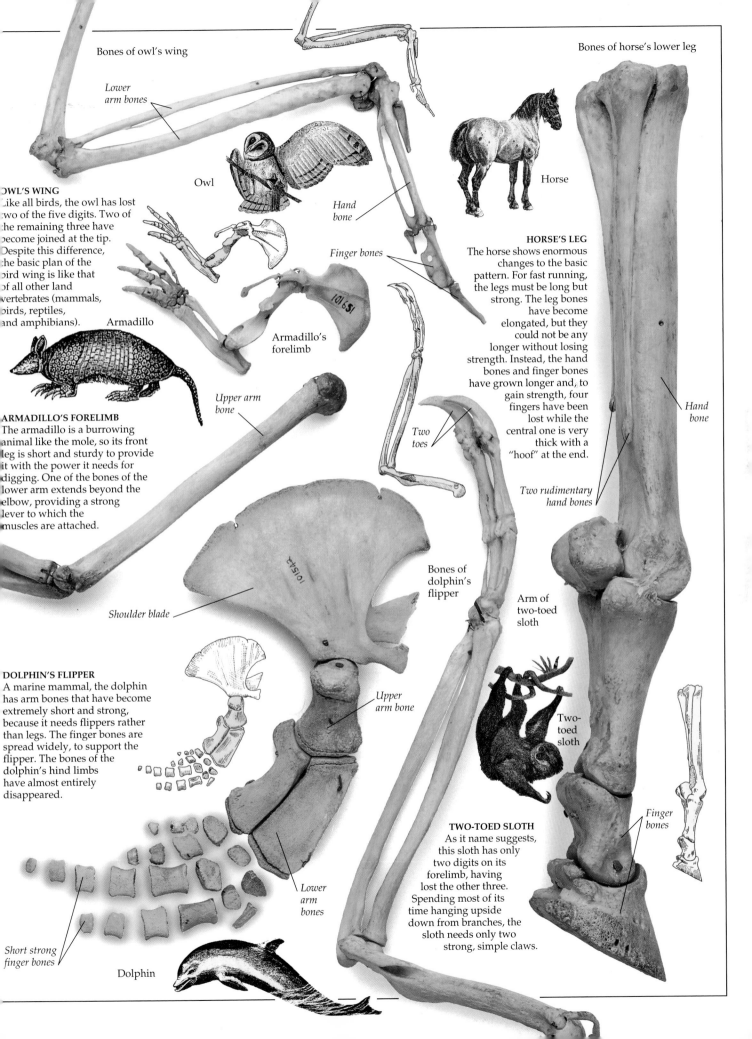

Bones of owl's wing

Lower arm bones

Owl

Hand bone

Finger bones

OWL'S WING
Like all birds, the owl has lost
two of the five digits. Two of
the remaining three have
become joined at the tip.
Despite this difference,
the basic plan of the
bird wing is like that
of all other land
vertebrates (mammals,
birds, reptiles,
and amphibians).

Armadillo

Armadillo's forelimb

ARMADILLO'S FORELIMB
The armadillo is a burrowing
animal like the mole, so its front
leg is short and sturdy to provide
it with the power it needs for
digging. One of the bones of the
lower arm extends beyond the
elbow, providing a strong
lever to which the
muscles are attached.

Upper arm bone

Bones of horse's lower leg

Horse

HORSE'S LEG
The horse shows enormous
changes to the basic
pattern. For fast running,
the legs must be long but
strong. The leg bones
have become
elongated, but they
could not be any
longer without losing
strength. Instead, the hand
bones and finger bones
have grown longer and, to
gain strength, four
fingers have been
lost while the
central one is very
thick with a
"hoof" at the end.

Hand bone

Two rudimentary hand bones

Two toes

Shoulder blade

DOLPHIN'S FLIPPER
A marine mammal, the dolphin
has arm bones that have become
extremely short and strong,
because it needs flippers rather
than legs. The finger bones are
spread widely, to support the
flipper. The bones of the
dolphin's hind limbs
have almost entirely
disappeared.

Upper arm bone

Bones of dolphin's flipper

Arm of two-toed sloth

Two-toed sloth

Finger bones

Lower arm bones

TWO-TOED SLOTH
As it name suggests,
this sloth has only
two digits on its
forelimb, having
lost the other three.
Spending most of its
time hanging upside
down from branches, the
sloth needs only two
strong, simple claws.

Short strong finger bones

Dolphin

Animal and plant distribution

IN DARWIN'S TIME, it was believed that each species had been created by God to suit best the conditions of a particular place. This "special creation" theory had many weak points, as Darwin made clear. In Australia mammals introduced from Europe had overrun the country, wiping out some native mammals. If Australian animals were exactly right for Australia, how could this happen? Darwin showed how migration and evolution could explain the patterns of distribution far better. Islands were an important part of his argument. The animals of the Cape Verde Islands are basically like those in Africa, and the Galapagos animals are like South American animals. Since these two island groups have much the same conditions, why had the Creator not made similar animals for them? Darwin suggested that animals and plants had arrived from the nearest mainland. Some had then evolved into unique types.

PLANT HUNTER
The botanist Joseph Hooker (1817-1911) searched for new plants in the Himalayas and New Zealand and was director of the Royal Botanic Gardens at Kew, near London. Darwin's good friend and colleague, he told him a great deal about plant distribution.

Thick bony plate from the outer coveri[ng] of a Glyptodon

ARMORED ANCESTOR
While in South America, Darwin found the remains of a *Glyptodon*, a prehistoric giant armored animal. He realized that it resembled the living armadillos of South America. This continuity between animals of the past and present had also been found in Australia, and it provided strong supporting evidence for the idea of evolution.

Fossilized skull of *Glyptodon*

Illustration of *Glyptodon*

ONCE ON AN ISLAND
The modern armadillo is just one of the many unusual mammals of South America. If animals and plants could travel freely, there should be roughly the same species everywhere, but in fact there are many blocks to migration, such as oceans, deserts, and mountain ranges. South America was an island for millions of years, and many unique mammals evolved there during this time.

Modern armadillo

Dried mud

Duck's foot

New Zealand

The animals on these islands are well explained by evolution. Strong sea currents prevented most mammals from getting there, so birds and insects, which arrived by air, evolved to fill some of the slots normally taken by mammal species.

New Zealand

MOAS AND KIWIS
The flightless kiwi is found only in New Zealand, as were the giant flightless birds called moas, which are now extinct. Moas and kiwis evolved from flying birds that colonized the islands of New Zealand millions of years ago.

Kiwi

Giant moa

Seedlings sprout from mud

GIANT CRICKET
Because there are no mice in New Zealand, the giant bush cricket, or weta, has evolved to fill the slot that mice occupy elsewhere. In general, mammals are less able to cross oceans than are birds, reptiles or insects.

GHOSTLY FOOT
The moas died out quite recently because of overhunting. Their undecayed remains (not fossils) are still sometimes found in caves. This is a foot from this enormous bird.

WANDERING PLANTS
How could plants travel to an island? This question was crucial for Darwin. He imagined that waterbirds, which fly long distances and rest on islands, might unintentionally transport plant seeds. He scraped dry mud from birds' feet and mixed it with water – seedlings sprang up, as he had expected.

Weta, life size

The Galapagos

Darwin's visit to the Galapagos islands provided him with some excellent evidence. In general, the animals of the islands resembled those of South America, but many species were unique to the Galapagos.

Map of Galapagos Islands from *A Naturalist's Voyage Round the World* by Darwin

Galapagos finches

DARWIN'S FINCHES
The Galapagos finches are clearly related to a type of finch from South America. Each of the 13 species has a differently shaped beak. The beaks are adapted to different kinds of food ranging from insects to seeds.

ATTACKED BY BIRDS
Henry Bates (1825-1892) helped Darwin by supplying him with data on animals and plants in the Amazon rain forest. Bates was one of many naturalists to study distant parts of the world for the first time, and Darwin sought information from several of them.

CHANCE LANDING
The Galapagos Islands are some 1,300 km (800 miles) from South America. All the Galapagos finches are probably descended from a small mainland flock that was blown off course and reached the islands millions of years ago.

Fossil evidence

DARWIN STUDIED the fossil record carefully for evidence that evolution had occurred. He found no strong evidence against the idea, and much evidence in favor, although the fossils certainly did not give a complete picture of the past. The gaps in the fossil record are still being studied today (p. 46). Looking at the fossil evidence in favor of evolution, some of the most interesting fossils are the mammal-like reptiles. These arose about 300 million years ago and became a large and very diverse group. Some of them gradually evolved into mammals during the dinosaur era, and the fossils that have been found form a complete series from reptile to mammal, with no major gaps. There are other sets of fossils that show similar gradual changes. Darwin believed he could explain the gaps in other parts of the fossil record, but he was greatly concerned about the seemingly sudden appearance of animal life on Earth some 570 million years ago, in the period known as the Cambrian (p. 60).

INSIDE STORY
Sliced in half, an ammonite reveals its intricate chambers.

Hand bones

Fragments of lower arm bones

Upper arm bone

Part of shoulder girdle

Ribs

Synapsid opening, seen only in mammals and mammal-like reptiles

ALMOST A MAMMAL
This is the fossilized skeleton of an animal called *Procynosuchus*, a type of mammal-like reptile known as a cynodont. It was from the cynodonts that the true mammals evolved, so they have more mammalian characters than their predecessors.

Lower jaw

Parts of shoulder girdle

Cambrian explosion

Darwin's answer to the problem of the sudden appearance of life in the Cambrian, the "Cambrian explosion," was to predict that, as more Precambrian rocks were explored, fossils would be found. This has indeed happened, but the finds consist mainly of fossils of bacteria – far too simple to be the immediate ancestors of the Cambrian animals. The only larger Precambrian creatures are a strange group called the Ediacara fauna (p. 47), but these do not look much like later creatures and probably died out entirely. No definite ancestors for the Cambrian animals have yet been found.

DIVERSE LIFE FORMS
These pieces of rock (left) are all from the Cambrian period, and they contain the remains of very different kinds of animals with shells – marine mollusks (far left), several kinds of trilobite, (center), and an animal called *Ridersia*. Their appearance in the fossil record is very sudden, and their immediate ancestors remain something of a mystery.

ANCIENT CELLS
The circles on this Precambrian rock are fossil colonies of cyanobacteria, or blue-green algae. To check that these were living things, scientists can now use chemical analysis of the rock, a technique unavailable for *Eozoon* (see right). With a scanning electron microscope, even the detail of their fine structure can now be seen.

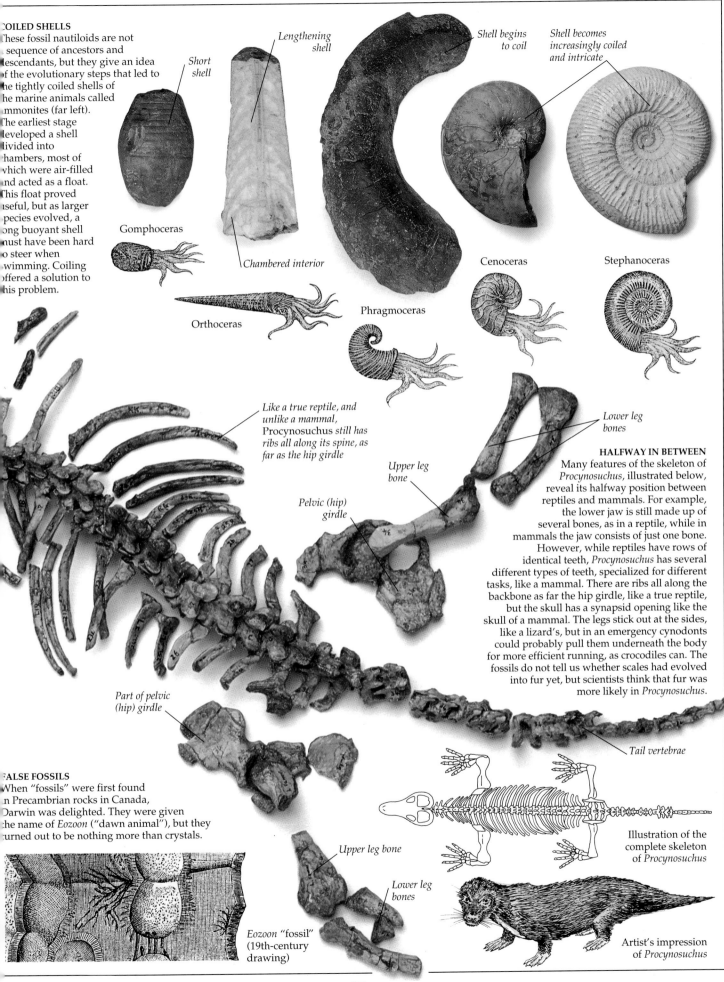

COILED SHELLS

These fossil nautiloids are not a sequence of ancestors and descendants, but they give an idea of the evolutionary steps that led to the tightly coiled shells of the marine animals called ammonites (far left). The earliest stage developed a shell divided into chambers, most of which were air-filled and acted as a float. This float proved useful, but as larger species evolved, a long buoyant shell must have been hard to steer when swimming. Coiling offered a solution to this problem.

Short shell

Lengthening shell

Shell begins to coil

Shell becomes increasingly coiled and intricate

Gomphoceras

Chambered interior

Orthoceras

Phragmoceras

Cenoceras

Stephanoceras

Like a true reptile, and unlike a mammal, Procynosuchus still has ribs all along its spine, as far as the hip girdle

Upper leg bone

Pelvic (hip) girdle

Lower leg bones

HALFWAY IN BETWEEN

Many features of the skeleton of *Procynosuchus*, illustrated below, reveal its halfway position between reptiles and mammals. For example, the lower jaw is still made up of several bones, as in a reptile, while in mammals the jaw consists of just one bone. However, while reptiles have rows of identical teeth, *Procynosuchus* has several different types of teeth, specialized for different tasks, like a mammal. There are ribs all along the backbone as far the hip girdle, like a true reptile, but the skull has a synapsid opening like the skull of a mammal. The legs stick out at the sides, like a lizard's, but in an emergency cynodonts could probably pull them underneath the body for more efficient running, as crocodiles can. The fossils do not tell us whether scales had evolved into fur yet, but scientists think that fur was more likely in *Procynosuchus*.

Part of pelvic (hip) girdle

Tail vertebrae

FALSE FOSSILS

When "fossils" were first found in Precambrian rocks in Canada, Darwin was delighted. They were given the name of *Eozoon* ("dawn animal"), but they turned out to be nothing more than crystals.

Upper leg bone

Lower leg bones

Eozoon "fossil" (19th-century drawing)

Illustration of the complete skeleton of *Procynosuchus*

Artist's impression of *Procynosuchus*

The age of the Earth

HAVING LOOKED AT THE EVIDENCE of fossils (p. 26) and of living things (pp. 22 and 24), Darwin became convinced that evolution had occurred. At the same time, he asked himself *how* it might have occurred. In 1838 he hit on his theory of natural selection (p. 36). An obvious feature of natural selection is that it could not work quickly, because it is haphazard rather than purposeful. Darwin knew that evolution through natural selection needed an enormous amount of time, but this did not worry him, as Charles Lyell's *Principles of Geology* had convinced him that the Earth was many hundreds of millions of years old. Since Lyell's time, geological research has confirmed his basic ideas, and he is known as the "father of modern geology." In 1866, however, the physicist William Thomson launched an attack on both Lyell and Darwin, claiming that the Earth was, at the most, 100 million years old. Later, his figure fell to 20 million years. His calculations were based on the rate of heat loss from the Earth, the present temperature of the outer crust, and the assumption that it had originally been molten. Darwin called this "one of my sorest troubles," and in later editions of *The Origin of Species* he played down natural selection, emphasizing other supposed mechanisms that he thought would work faster. Not until 1904 did Thomson's fundamental error become clear.

SLOW FORCES
The geological theories of Charles Lyell (1797-1875) were a reaction against Cuvier's catastrophe theories (p. 16). Lyell set out to explain geology using only forces that were still at work, rather than relying on ancient and unimaginable catastrophes, as Cuvier did. Since present-day forces work very slowly, the Earth must be very old, Lyell claimed.

Geological map of the Weald from the 19th century

Cross section through the Weald

THE AGE OF THE WEALD
Darwin's interest in the age of the Earth and how it might be estimated led to some experiments and calculations of his own. The area of southern England where he lived, called the Weald, consists of layers of sediment that were laid down under the sea, later forced upward into mountains, and then eroded away. Darwin tried to work out the age of the Weald by estimating its original height and the rate of erosion. The rate was too slow, and his date of 300 million years was wildly wrong. The Weald is only 20-30 million years old.

Worm stone set up at Downe House, Darwin's home

THE WORM STONE
Darwin's interest in time and how it changed the Earth took a new turn with his studies of earthworms (p. 21). He suspected that the action of worms in the soil would slowly bury buildings. To measure the speed of this, he placed a millstone on his lawn, and this special instrument was made to measure how far the stone sank each year.

Pivot

Stand

Micrometer to measure movement of stone

Rods set deep in ground

Ring to rest on worm stone

Early Geiger counter, used to measure radioactivity

Mica window

Gas-filled copper cylinder

Electrical supply

WRONG ANSWER
Radioactive emissions were discovered in 1896, and in 1903 Pierre Curie found that radium salts constantly give out heat, warming the Earth's crust. Thomson was unaware of this, and it made his calculation of the Earth's age entirely wrong. However, he made the arrogant claim that physics was a superior science to geology or biology. He thought that his one calculation could therefore overrule all the evidence collected by Lyell and by Darwin.

ASTRONOMER SON
George Darwin (1845-1913), one of Charles's 10 children, was a mathematician and astronomer. Asked by his father to check Thomson's calculations about the age of the Earth, he concluded that they were mathematically correct. In later life, George Darwin was among the first to recognize that radioactivity was constantly warming the Earth's crust, making Thomson's calculations meaningless.

LORD KELVIN
William Thomson (1824-1907) was a British physicist who later became Lord Kelvin. He and his followers had some religious motives for attacking Darwin. Like many other people, they disliked the fact that natural selection showed no purpose or direction.

Insulated handle

RADIOMETRIC DATING
Radioactive elements in rocks now allow them to be dated accurately. Each radioactive element breaks down at a constant rate and always forms the same product. For example, potassium 40, found in volcanic rocks, breaks down to give argon 40. The older the rock, the more argon 40 there is. The Earth's original rocks have long ago been worn away by wind and rain, but by using the age of the oldest rocks on Earth (3,900 million years) and estimating rates of erosion, geologists have calculated that the Earth is 4,500 million years old.

MOON ROCK
Rock samples brought back from the Moon have proved useful to geologists. The Moon and Earth were formed at the same time but, as there is no atmosphere on the Moon, there is no erosion. As predicted, geologists' calculations make Moon rock 4,500 million years old.

DATES CONFIRMED
Meteorites were formed at the same time as the Earth. Radiometric dating shows that they are 4,500 million years old. The ages of Moon rock and meteorites have both confirmed the age of the Earth that was calculated by modern geologists.

Artificial selection

As part of his search for evidence about evolution, Darwin looked at domesticated animals and plants. During his lifetime, great progress had been made in developing new varieties of plants and animals through "artificial selection" or "selective breeding." This involves choosing those individals that have the desired qualities and breeding only from them, rejecting the rest. Knowing the extent to which certain species of plants and animals had been improved in the preceding 50 years, Darwin argued that far greater changes were possible over thousands of years. This made him suspect that all breeds of sheep, for example, were descended from a single ancestor. Other naturalists disagreed – they thought that every breed must have come from a different wild species. One naturalist even suggested that there had once been *eleven* different species of wild sheep in Britain, found nowhere else in the world. Darwin pointed out how unlikely this was, since all Britain's living mammals are also found in Europe. Subsequent evidence has shown that Darwin was correct: all the different breeds of sheep were indeed developed by selective breeding from just one ancestor. The same is true of other domesticated animals, such as cows, dogs, and horses.

ROCK DOVE
This wild bird is the raw material with which pigeon breeders began. All the different pigeon breeds kept in captivity are descended from it.

DARWIN'S HOBBY
As well as his horse, Darwin kept rabbits, chickens, ducks, and pigeons. He crossed all the different breeds of pigeon and was surprised that the young often had the same colors as the rock dove, even if neither parent had them. He realized that the rock dove must be the ancestor of them all.

PIGEON BREEDS
These are some of the many different breeds of pigeon that Darwin studied. He felt that if so much change could come about through selective breeding, then similar changes could occur through the action of natural forces alone.

ANCIENT CATTLE
Wall paintings in the tombs of Ancient Egypt show cattle of many different breed Some naturalists saw such paintings as evidence that every breed was descended from a different species. After all, these breeds already existed thousands of years ago. Darwin argued that there was no reason to assume that the Egyptians were the first farmers – selective breeding could have begun even earlier. There is now ample evidence that his idea was correct.

GIANT DOG
The Irish wolfhound is one of the largest dogs: it can be 39 in (1 m) tall at the shoulder. The smallest, the chihuahua, may stand only 8 in (20 cm) tall. Studies of their DNA (p. 52) show that all breeds of dog are descended from the European wolf.

TAIL-FREE CAT
The Manx cat has been bred to have no tail. Cats are more difficult to breed selectively than dogs, as they like to roam at night and mate as they please. Many dog breeds were developed for useful purposes, which explains why they are more varied than cats.

Irish wolfhound

Cherry tomatoes

BIG, BIGGER
Plant breeders can easily produce smaller or larger breeds, as these tomatoes show. The ancestral plant has been found in South America, and its tiny "tomato" is no larger than a red currant.

BALD DOG
The Chinese crested dog is virtually naked except for long wisps of hair on its head and tail. Breeders can alter the temperament, size, shape, and color of a dog. Its coat can be made long or short, straight or curly.

Chinese crested dog

Giant tomato

Yellow tomato

STRANGE FRUIT
Yellow tomatoes and red grapefruit are just two of the oddly colored fruits created by plant breeders. Darwin was convinced that artificial selection indicated a way in which evolution could occur – through a process that he called natural selection (p. 36).

SEEDLESS PRODUCE
In nature, fruits exist solely to distribute seeds. If there are no seeds inside it, a young fruit will normally wither and die. Breeders have managed to overcome this so that certain fruits, including bananas, some grapes, and some oranges, have no seeds.

Seedless orange

Seedless grapes

Pink grapefruit

All cultivated bananas are seedless

Variation and inheritance

By 1837 CHARLES DARWIN was certain that evolution had taken place, and he was thinking hard about the driving force behind it. For a time, he thought that Lamarck's theory about striving for change (p. 12) was the answer, but Darwin soon saw its weak points. He began taking an interest in anything that might answer this difficult question, including the breeding of crop plants, farm animals, and pets (p. 30). By questioning breeders, he learned that there were small variations between individuals, which the breeders picked out. A dog breeder would choose a feature and cross two dogs carrying it. From the puppies, those that had inherited the chosen feature would be picked out and bred. If this was repeated for several generations, the feature became more and more pronounced. Darwin saw that a similar process could occur in the wild, and he called it "natural selection" (p. 36). The three ingredients needed were variation, inheritance, and competition. Inheritance clearly took place, although Darwin never really understood how. Variation between individuals was also apparent. The third factor, competition, or "the struggle for existence," was also a fact of nature (p. 34). Competition in the wild had the same role as the dog breeder, "selecting" particular individuals for breeding and discarding others.

NO TWO THE SAME
Variation is shown in the shell colors and patterns of a seashore mollusk, *Nerites*. Not all variation is as obvious as this. There may be very small variations in size or shell thickness that are not noticeable, but that affect the animal's survival. Studies of internal features show even more differences between individuals.

Varied *Nerites* shells

Normal teasel

MUTANT TEASEL
Fuller's teasel is a mutant form of the teasel plant that has curved spines on the seed head instead of straight ones. Mutants were observed in the 19th century, but only in the 20th century were they studied systematically by geneticists (p. 51). Mutants arise through a sudden change, or mutation, in the DNA. This change occurs because the DNA is copied inaccurately when the reproductive cells are being produced (p. 53). Mutations are not dictated by the needs of the plant or animal. In fact, most mutations are damaging, and the mutants die young. But a few mutations are useful, and these are a major source of the variation on which natural selection operates.

Fuller's teasel

CHANGING BUTTERFLY
Variation is obvious in the small copper butterfly. Depending on circumstances, some may do better than others. For example, in a cool summer the darker butterflies warm up more quickly in the sun, as darker colors are better absorbers of heat.

Darwin and heredity

Darwin's greatest problem was heredity. He believed, wrongly, that acquired characteristics (p. 13) are inherited. But, unlike Lamarck, Darwin did not make this the cornerstone of his theory. He thought that random variation and selection were more important. Darwin's more significant mistake was to think that the characteristics of the parents would blend in the offspring. He could see that if inheritance did involve the blending of characteristics, this would be an obstacle to evolution by natural selection, because if one parent had a useful new characteristic it would be diluted in the offspring. Despite this, he could think of no alternative.

Normal young

Albino young

COLOR CLUE
Darwin knew that when albino and normal mice are crossed, the colors do not blend in the young. He found several other examples, but thought they were just oddities, exceptions to the rule. In fact they held the key to heredity, as Mendel showed (p. 51).

FAMILY TRAITS
Inheritance is obvious in most families. However, children often do not look like their parents; rather, they resemble their grandparents or other relatives. Darwin was puzzled by this, but geneticists later realized that "dominant" and "recessive" genes (p. 51) were responsible.

Normal
father Dwarf
Russian hamster

Albino
mother Dwarf
Russian hamster

The struggle for existence

MANY ANIMALS lay hundreds of eggs every year. Very few of these live to become adults – a fact that is obvious to any naturalist. The poet, Alfred Lord Tennyson was aware of this when, in 1833, he wrote "Are God and Nature then at strife, That Nature lends such evil dreams? So careful of the type she seems, So careless of the single life." Unlike Tennyson, most people preferred to ignore the facts and see nature as happy and harmonious, a view made popular by the Reverend William Paley (p. 38). Darwin knew that plants and animals died in great numbers, but it took years for him to realize that this loss of life could be the driving force behind evolution. A naturalist and clergyman, the Reverend Thomas Malthus, helped him see the light. In 1798 Malthus had published *An Essay on the Principle of Population*, which argued that all living things tend to increase far faster than food supplies and that, in the case of humans, numbers are only kept in check by famine and disease. These ideas were well known to Darwin, but he did not actually read Malthus's essay until 1838. As soon as he read it, the idea of natural selection (p. 36) came to him in a flash, enabling him to make sense of all his earlier observations. Nevertheless, Darwin was always troubled by the "wasteful works of Nature." He consoled himself with the thought that "the war of nature is not incessant, that no fear is felt, that death is generally prompt, and that the vigorous, the healthy, and the happy survive and multiply."

STARVING THE POOR
The Reverend Thomas Malthus (1766-1834) was a kindly man, but his essay inspired a brutal new Poor Law in Britain. The law took welfare support away from the poor unless they went into prisonlike "workhouses" where husbands and wives were separated. Feeding poor people, according to Malthus, only made poverty worse in the long run, because the poor then had more children

Tufted seeds

Dandelion flower

LUCK AND SURVIVAL
A single dandelion flower produces dozens of seeds. The wind blows them away, and there is no guarantee that they will land on soil where they can flourish. Most never grow into plants. Chance clearly plays the major part in deciding which seeds arrive in a good spot. But for those that survive this stage, new struggles begin: struggles for moisture, light, and space. In these contests, chance plays less of a part, and the plant's own qualities become more important.

Dandelion "clock" with dry seeds ready to disperse

Dandelion head after the seeds have been blown away

Dozens of seeds from a single head

HUNTER AND PREY
A thin and hungry polar bear pursues a nimble arctic fox across the snow. One of the most important parts of the struggle for survival is the need to eat – and the need to avoid being eaten by others.

FIGHTING FOR SPACE
Like most seabirds, gannets are vulnerable to predators when nesting, so they nest only on small, rocky islands where there are no rats or foxes to destroy their eggs and young. As suitable islands are few, they become very crowded. Competition between animals for nesting sites is another aspect of the "struggle for existence."

Froglets set off into the wide world

Eggs

Frog's spawn

RED IN TOOTH AND CLAW
The poet Alfred Lord Tennyson wrote his poem *In Memoriam* in 1833, 25 years before Darwin published *The Origin of Species*. It includes the memorable line "Nature red in tooth and claw." This phrase later came to symbolize people's hatred for the idea of natural selection. They reacted as if Darwin had invented the struggle for existence, rather than simply described it.

THE NUMBERS GAME
A frog can lay hundreds of eggs in a single year. If all these survived to adulthood and produced young of their own, the world would be knee-deep in frogs within 10 years. Clearly, most of them die. Some of the eggs and tadpoles are killed by fungi, some by predators. Others die from lack of food. Of the few dozen froglets that may survive each year, only one or two are likely to live long enough to breed.

Adult frog

Natural selection

HOW DOES EVOLUTION OCCUR? Charles Darwin's answer was through "natural selection." He realized that there was always some variation between individuals within a species (p. 32), so that some are a little larger, some have thicker fur, or slightly longer legs. He also realized that there is a struggle for existence (p. 34) because more individuals are born than can survive. To some extent, chance plays a part in deciding which ones survive, but the characteristics of the individual must sometimes make a difference. The animal with longer legs will run faster and thus escape a predator. The animal with thicker fur will survive a cold winter. Only those that survive have the chance to produce young ones – and that is where inheritance (p. 33) is important. If the slightly longer legs or thicker fur are passed on to some of the offspring, then more animals have those useful characteristics in the next generation. After hundreds of generations, these small changes may add up to a large and noticeable difference. Darwin proposed that this process produces adaptation (p. 38) and could also produce new species, given enough time (p. 40). The idea of natural selection came to Darwin in 1838, but he spent a further 20 years working on the idea and collecting more evidence. He was nervous about the controversies that his theory might provoke, and this too made him delay publication. Had Alfred Wallace (above left) not reached similar conclusions, Darwin might never have published at all.

WINTER KILLS
Killed by the cold and lack of food, this eagle has lost forever its chance of producing young. Another eagle, with thicker feathers, or better hunting abilities, may survive to produce chicks next spring.

Moths on light bark

Industrial pollution in 19th century England

CONCEALING COLORS
In the 19th century a good example of natural selection occurred in the industrial regions of northern England, although no one grasped its significance at the time. The peppered moth rests on tree trunks by day. Its pale dappled wings are well camouflaged against lichens growing on the trunks, and this protects the moth from insect-eating birds. Pollution kills off lichens, and as industry grew, the tree trunks were turning black with soot from factory smokestacks. Dark versions of the peppered moth arose by mutation (p. 32) and were better camouflaged than the original form. Gradually, the dark forms became more and more common.

Moths on dark bark

Sexual selection

Apart from natural selection, Darwin also identified another important mechanism: sexual selection. When animals mate, they are choosy about their partners. Usually it is the female choosing the male, or males fighting to control females. Sometimes, however, females must compete for males, or both partners may be choosy. The qualities that ensure success differ widely, from physical strength to bright feathers. Only those chosen as mates pass on their characteristics to the next generation.

Single tail feather from male peacock

Flowers

Well-fed plant with plentiful flowers that will produce more seeds and thus more offspring

FIGHTING FOR MATES
Male elephant seals fight for the right to breed. On the beaches where they come to breed every year, only a few males gain a territory. These territory-holders, the ones who can fight off their rivals, herd together a "harem" of females and mate with all of them. This type of sexual selection produces great size and strength in the males. The female seals are less than half their size.

Vigorous growth

How does it begin?

It is easy to see how natural selection can make fur thicker or legs longer, but how does a totally new feature develop? In every case, there must be something for natural selection to work on, an existing feature that can be modified to make the new one.

Few flowers

APPEALING TAIL
Sexual selection often involves males attracting females. Peacocks display their tails to females, who choose the best-looking male. Bright feathers may originally have been favored because they showed that a male was healthy, but once this process begins, the feathers may become more and more elaborate.

Unfed plant

Meat being placed on leaf

HUNGRY PLANTS
The leaves of the sundew plant have evolved to become insect traps. Most plant leaves can absorb some nutrients directly, and this must have been the starting point for the ancestor of sundews. They grew in bogs with poor soil, and small insects that happened to drown on their damp leaves would have supplied extra minerals. Natural selection would then have favored plants that increased this nutrient supply. If a plant with stickier leaves appeared, it would do better than others, because small flies would become stuck on the leaves. Darwin experimented with sundews, feeding some with small pieces of meat and keeping others unfed. Those fed on meat grew more quickly, produced more flowers, and set more seeds. He had shown that being able to trap and digest insects would be a characteristic favoured by natural selection.

Understanding adaptation

William Paley
(1743-1805)

MOLES HAVE STRONG, BROAD FRONT FEET for digging through soil. Ducks have webbed feet for swimming. Polar bears have very thick fur. It is clear to any naturalist that all plants and animals are superbly adapted to their climate and way of life. Darwin proposed that these adaptations were an outcome of natural selection. However, there was already a powerful and popular theory about adaptation known as "natural theology." This interpreted all adaptation as evidence of the creator's handiwork. *Natural Theology, or Evidences of the Existence and Attributes of the Deity*, by the English clergyman William Paley, set out the ideas most fully. Published in 1802, Paley's book was widely read. While studying for the clergy as a young man, Darwin had read and admired it, not thinking that he would one day be its greatest critic. Fortunately, the two opposing theories can each be tested against the facts. Natural theology predicts that all adaptations should be perfect. Evolution through natural selection predicts that they should be influenced by (and often limited by) the past.

PALEY'S WATCH
William Paley began *Natural Theology* with an example to prove his basic point. He imagined himself walking across a field and finding a watch among the stones. Unlike the stones, the watch has moving parts that work together for a purpose. The existence of the watch would prove that there was a watchmaker. Paley drew a parallel between a watch and an animal. Just as the watch proved the existence of a watchmaker, so an animal (or a plant) proved the existence of a Creator. By studying natural history, the nature of God could be better understood.

Faces of leaf-nosed bats

What purpose?

Inspired by natural theology, naturalists set out to find God's intended "purpose" for each living thing, a difficult task, especially in the case of pests such as rats and fleas. In Darwin's view, the only "purpose" of any creature is a private one - to survive and produce young. If it does this, it has succeeded in passing on its characteristics to the next generation.

ECHOES OF CREATION?
Bats navigate by making high-pitched sounds and listening for the echoes. Some have elaborate nose-leaves to channel the sound. Can such devices be produced by natural selection, or must there be a "watchmaker," a creator? The fact is that there are many simple versions of this "radar" among bats, and a range of intermediate forms leading up to the most complex ones. This has convinced biologists that such features can, and have, evolved.

European mole

Long, thin hand and finger bones support wing

SAME BONES
The bat's spreading wing and the mole's stubby digging arm have the same set of bones, as do the arms of all mammals (p. 23). This astonishing similarity only makes sense if Darwin was correct and they come from the same distant ancestor.

Strong arm for digging

Leaf-nosed bat

Far from perfect

According to Natural Theology, the adaptations of living things should be perfect. According to Darwin, adaptations are always restricted by the ancestry of the plant or animal, because natural selection can only work on the raw material available. If the raw material is not ideal for the purpose, or natural selection has not had long enough to work, the adaptations will be less-than-perfect.

Panda's paw

Bear attacking animal

THE PANDA'S THUMB
Bears are carnivores, and their paws have five very short "fingers." Giant pandas, descended from bears, eat bamboo shoots and need a thumb to hold them. In fact, they have evolved one, but it is a short, imperfect thumb jutting out from the wrist. It seems that the bear's paw was too specialised for natural selection to "reverse" the basic plan and make a true thumb. Instead, the panda's false thumb has grown from a bone in the wrist.

False thumb

STILL ADAPTING
Many people suffer from backache, or problems with their hips, knees, or feet, while pain in the arms is rare. In Darwin's terms, this makes sense. Humans are unusual among mammals in standing upright. The molecular evidence (p. 54) suggests that we only began to do so between 5 and 8 million years ago. The human back and legs have not yet had time to adapt fully.

Frigate bird

Giant panda

Human spine

FRIGATE BIRD PUZZLE
Darwin pointed out that both frigate birds and geese have webbed feet, yet neither goes into the water. He explained their feet as a leftover from their past, both being descended from waterbirds. If they were designed by a creator, Darwin wondered, why did they have these useless features?

DESIGN FAULT
Loons, or divers, can scarcely walk on land (below), because their legs are set so far back on the body. Most diving birds have the legs set well back, because this is the best position for efficient swimming. The penguin (left) has solved the problem of walking by adopting an upright stance. For the loon, upright walking may evolve in time. A "watchmaker" might have made the loon more mobile on land by standing it upright, or by adding another pair of legs near the middle.

King penguin

Red-throated diver

How new species are formed

ALTHOUGH DARWIN called his book *The Origin of Species*, he said very little about how new species might arise. In fact, he called this the "mystery of mysteries." Today the process is better understood, although there are still disagreements about the details. In general, most new species arise when a population becomes cut off from the rest of its kind, especially if it then lives in conditions that differ from those of the parent species. This might happen, for example, when birds are blown off course and reach distant islands (p. 25) or cross a mountain range. Sheer distance can also be a physical barrier, as in the case of a ring species (below). Under new conditions, or simply because they are isolated, the population may begin to evolve in a different direction and may develop into a new race or subspecies. In time, that subspecies can change so much and become so different from the rest of its species that the two can no longer interbreed. Once this happens, they are two distinct species. Occasionally, a new species may arise in other ways, without any geographical isolation.

THE COMTE DE BUFFON
Georges Buffon (1707-1788) of France was the first to define a species as a group of living things that can all potentially interbreed with each other, but not with members of other species.

Herring gull
(*Larus argentatus argentatus*)

Lesser black-backed gull (*Larus fuscus graellsi*)

ONE SPECIES OR TWO?
The herring gull (left) and the lesser black-backed gull (right) are descended from gulls that lived in eastern Siberia. These ancestral gulls spread out to both east and west. In time, the two lines of migration met on the other side of the globe, over northern Europe. The two ends of this circle are the herring gull and the lesser black-backed gull. These birds have changed so much from their common ancestor that they do not interbreed, except very rarely.

RING SPECIES
Each of the different subspecies of herring gull interbreeds with its neighbors, as do the different subspecies of lesser black-backed gull. In eastern Siberia, the herring gulls interbreed with neighbors that are called black-backed gulls, but could just as well be called herring gulls. These gulls form a "ring species" and show how new species can arise through accumulated small changes.

Larus argentatus vegae

Larus argentatus birulaii

North Pole

Larus argentatus smithsonianus

Larus fuscus antellus

Larus fuscus heuglini

Larus argentatus omissus

Larus fuscus fuscus

Larus argentatus argentatus

Larus fuscus graellsi

Isolating mechanisms

A new species may develop in isolation, but often it moves back into the area where the parent species lives. The two species may still be similar enough to mate and produce young, although these hybrid offspring are infertile (unable to have young themselves). For the parents, producing such a hybrid is a waste of time and energy, so it pays them to recognize their own species. They do so using signals such as smell, sound, color, or behavior. These signals, which keep species apart, are called "isolating mechanisms."

Chiffchaff   Wood warbler   Willow warbler

NOT ONE, BUT THREE
The English naturalist Gilbert White (1720-1793) was the first to notice that the chiffchaff, the willow warbler, and the wood warbler were three different species, and not just one. The wood warbler is slightly larger and brighter in color, but the chiffchaff and willow warbler look almost exactly the same. The songs of these three, however, are all distinctly different. For the birds, the songs are used by the female to select a mate, so in this way they act as an isolating mechanism, separating the otherwise similar species.

CHOOSING A MATE
Butterflies, which fly by day, recognize potential mates by their patterns and colors. Moths, which fly by night, rely more on scent. For many species, there are also internal mechanisms that prevent fertilization between different species. These are especially important in plants.

South American Sweet Oil butterflies mating

GETTING IT RIGHT
These butterflies have made the right choice of mate, but this is not always the case. Mistakes are occasionaly made because isolating mechanisms, like adapatations (p. 39), are a product of evolutionary change and are not necessarily perfect. For example, a horse may mate with a donkey, producing a mule, which is infertile.

Asian swallowtails mating

PERFUMED PARTNERS
Mice and many other mammals recognize their own species by characteristic scents. In some species, specific courtship rituals are performed. These are used to confirm that the correct choice of partner has been made.

KEPT APART
Theodosius Dobzhansky (1900-1975) worked with T.H. Morgan on fruit flies (p. 51) and helped in the synthesis of genetics and evolutionary theory. He coined the term "isolating mechanisms" for the biological barriers that discourage crossing between different species.

Living intermediates

GRADUAL GLIDING
Flying squirrels do not really fly, but glide from tree to tree. Gliding animals could have gradually evolved from ordinary tree dwellers by acquiring flaps of skin that broke their fall when jumping. Some gliders could then have evolved into flying animals such as birds and bats.

DARWIN BELIEVED THAT natural selection could produce adaptations (p. 38), but could it produce animals with a completely different way of life? Could it turn a marine animal into a land animal, or a nonflier into a flier? How might such major alterations be achieved through a series of small changes? Some transitional fossils have been found that help answer this question (p. 44), and "living intermediates" help make sense of the fossils. These living forms, such as lungfish and egg-laying mammals, are not the ancestors of other animals living today, but they may be related to those ancestors or may have followed a similar evolutionary path. In the case of lungfish, comparisons with fossils show that many extinct lungfish and other air-breathing fish flourished 380 million years ago. The climate was hot and dry, so pools and streams may have been shrinking and stagnant. Lungs must have evolved to allow fish to gulp air at the surface. Much later, some air-breathing fish probably began emerging on to the land briefly, to feed on the plentiful insects. They had fleshy fins, unlike most modern fish, and in time these must have evolved into legs. This case is typical of transitions: one feature (lungs) evolves for a particular purpose, but this paves the way for a further development (emergence on to land to feed), which then leads to the evolution of another feature (legs). A similar bit-by-bit transition is seen in birds. By looking at dinosaur and *Archaeopteryx* fossils (p. 45), and comparing living gliders such as flying squirrels, scientists can work out the gradual steps that led first to feathers, then to gliding, and finally to flight.

ASA GRAY (1810-1888)
American evolutionist Asa Gray also considered the problem of intermediates. Darwin wrote to him, "The eye to this day gives me a cold shudder, but when I think of the known fine gradations, my reason tells me I ought to conquer the cold shudder." Objectors to evolution claimed that the human eye could not have evolved by steps, but living intermediates show that it could.

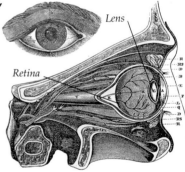

Lens

Retina

FINE GRADATIONS
The simplest eyes are just clumps of light-sensitive cells. Found in snails, they can do no more than distinguish light from dark. In higher animals, a transparent lens has evolved to focus light on to these light-sensitive cells, which now form the retina.

AUSTRALIAN LUNGFISH (*below*)
Lungfish, of which there are now only six species, can gulp air at the surface, allowing them to live in stagnant water containing little oxygen. Lungfish and other air-breathing fish flourished 380 million years ago when stagnant pools were probably a common feature of the landscape.

FLYING FISH
Darwin observed that flying fish "now glide far through the air, slightly rising and turning by the aid of their fluttering fins." If they had evolved into true fliers, Darwin asked, who would then have imagined that "in an early transitional state they had used their incipient organs of flight [fins] exclusively to escape being devoured by other fish?"

OBJECTION EXPLODED

Bombardier beetles are often claimed as the downfall of Darwinism. For defense, they produce an explosion of hot toxic liquid. Anti-evolutionists claim that the explosion occurs when two chemicals are mixed, and that each chemical alone is useless. This is incorrect. The chemicals are produced together, and they react only when acted on by enzymes. The chemicals and the enzymes have other uses in living bodies and are not made for this reaction alone. In other words, they were already available to be worked on by natural selection. Likely intermediate stages can be imagined in which toxic liquids were produced but without any explosion.

Bombardier beetle

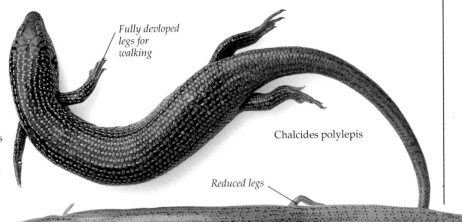

Fully devloped legs for walking

Chalcides polylepis

Both chemicals produced in this gland

Enzymes produced here

Diagram of defense system

Storage chamber for chemicals

Explosive blast

Explosion chamber

Cross-section through beetle

Reduced legs

Sphenops sepsoides

Chalcides chalcides

SKINKS LOSING LEGS

Among the skinks, every stage can be seen in the course of evolution that leads from a normal lizard to a legless one. This shows how snakes may gradually have evolved from a reptile ancestor with legs. The first stage seems to involve the legs getting smaller but remaining useful for running. These skinks can do without their legs when they choose to, and move like a snake. They simply straighten the legs and hold them flat against the body. This allows them to wriggle through long grass, or into a narrow crack in a rock.

Tiny leg

Remains of leg

Chalcides guentheri

EGG-LAYING MAMMALS

Spiny anteaters are not the direct ancestors of mammals, but they give a good indication of how mammals evolved. They show that being warm-blooded, having fur, and producing milk came before bearing live young. The existence of egg-laying mammals backs up the evidence from fossils (p. 26) that mammals evolved from reptiles. Other sources of evidence, such as comparisons of anatomy (p. 23) or of DNA and proteins (p. 54), tell the same story of a reptile-mammal link. The fact that all the different forms of evidence support each other suggests that evolution is more than just a theory.

Baby spiny anteater in mother's pouch

Reptile-like egg of spiny anteater

Spiny anteater

Fossil intermediates

Artist's impression of *Miacis* from 50 million years ago

LIKE LIVING INTERMEDIATES (p. 42), fossil intermediates can reveal how new groups evolved from existing ones. They are not a perfect guide, however, because the full set of intermediates is very rarely found. It has been estimated that only one fossil species is found for every 20,000 species that have lived, so the chances of finding an actual ancestor of a living group is very small. The most that scientists can hope for is to find a fossil species that was related to such an ancestor. This means that some guesswork must be used in reconstructing past events. However, the guesses made are based on a great deal of careful study of the fossils, and of living things. All ideas about how things evolved are repeatedly tested and questioned by other scientists. When new fossils are found, they are used to test existing theories about the past and may confirm or disprove those theories. Among the fossils that have helped to reveal the course of evolution are those of early frogs (below). Fossil frogs show that broad skulls came before features such as very long legs. Broad skulls and mouths are typical of animals that catch fast-moving prey underwater, so it seems that this led the way in frog evolution.

ANCIENT ELEPHANT
Together with other fossils, the 35 million-year-old fossil *Phiomia* (pictured in this artist's impression) shows how elephants, mammoths, and mastodons evolved from relatively small, hippolike animals.

HALFWAY THERE
Fossil skeletons of *Miacis* show that it was on the evolutionary line leading to martens and weasels. Fossils of *Miacis* have been found in coal seams, the remains of ancient dense forests, in Germany.

Artist's impression of 20-million-year old *Enaliarctos*

ANCIENT SEA DOG
Another fossil, *Enaliarctos*, reveals how doglike ancestors evolved into sea lions. It probably fed in the sea, but spent more time on land than living sea lions.

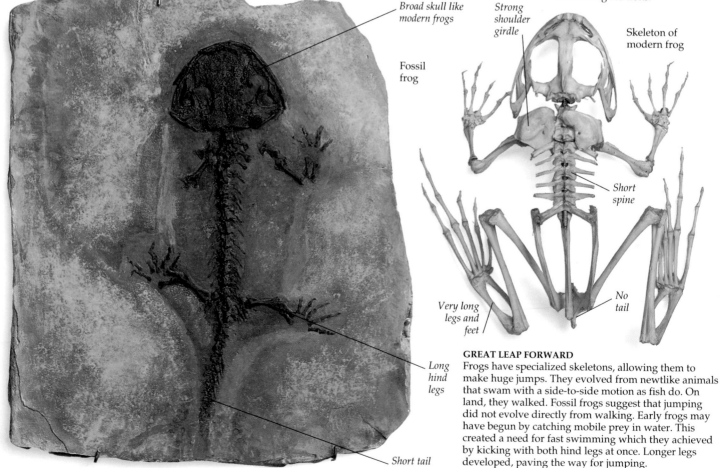

Broad skull like modern frogs

Fossil frog

Strong shoulder girdle

Skeleton of modern frog

Short spine

No tail

Very long legs and feet

Long hind legs

Short tail

GREAT LEAP FORWARD
Frogs have specialized skeletons, allowing them to make huge jumps. They evolved from newtlike animals that swam with a side-to-side motion as fish do. On land, they walked. Fossil frogs suggest that jumping did not evolve directly from walking. Early frogs may have begun by catching mobile prey in water. This created a need for fast swimming which they achieved by kicking with both hind legs at once. Longer legs developed, paving the way for jumping.

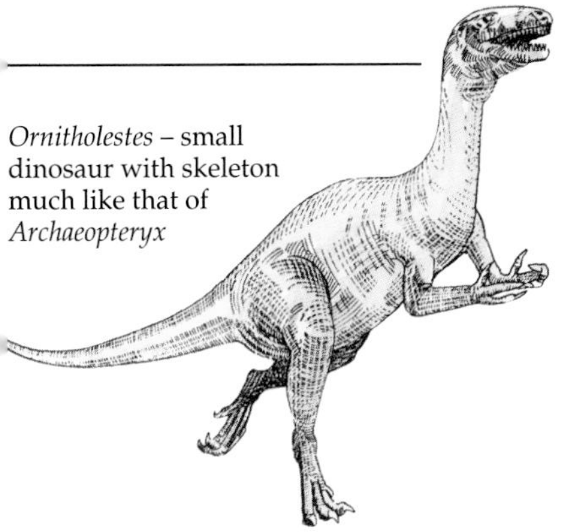

Ornitholestes – small dinosaur with skeleton much like that of *Archaeopteryx*

Wing feathers

Wing feathers

FROM DINOSAUR TO BIRD

The fossil *Archaeopteryx* is probably a close relative of the ancestor of birds, and shows how birds may have evolved. Its skeleton was very similar to some small dinosaurs, but it also had feathers. *Archaeopteryx* probably could not fly – it lacks a keel on its breastbone, the broad flattened extension to which the flight muscles are attached in modern birds. *Archaeopteryx* was probably a tree climber and glider. It may have hunted flying insects, or perhaps it just saved energy by swooping from tree to tree. In the ancestors of birds, gliding could have evolved into flight.

Wing bones

Wing bones

Leg bones

Part of spine

Tail bones

Foot

Artist's impression of *Archaeopteryx* gliding

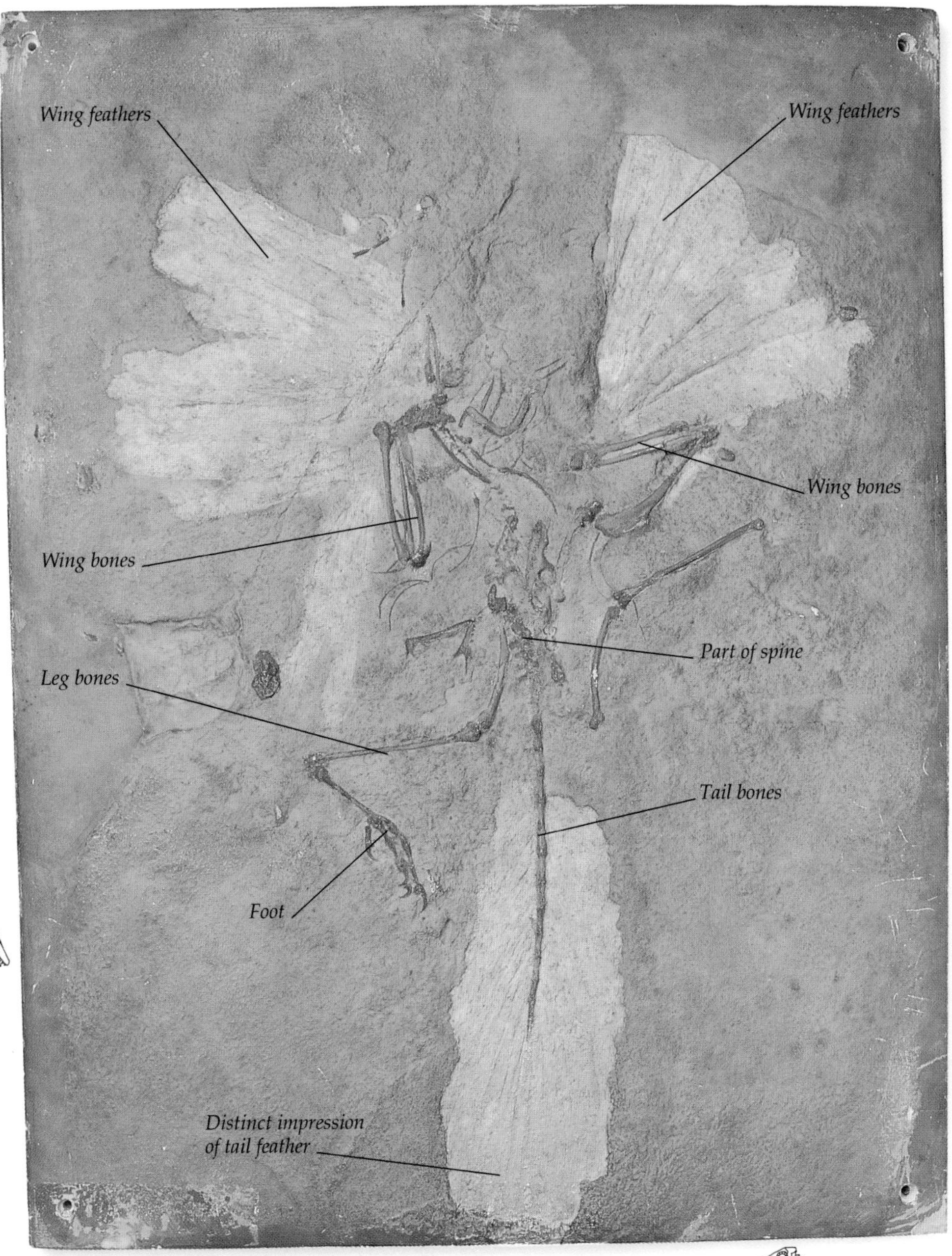

Fossil of *Archaeopteryx*

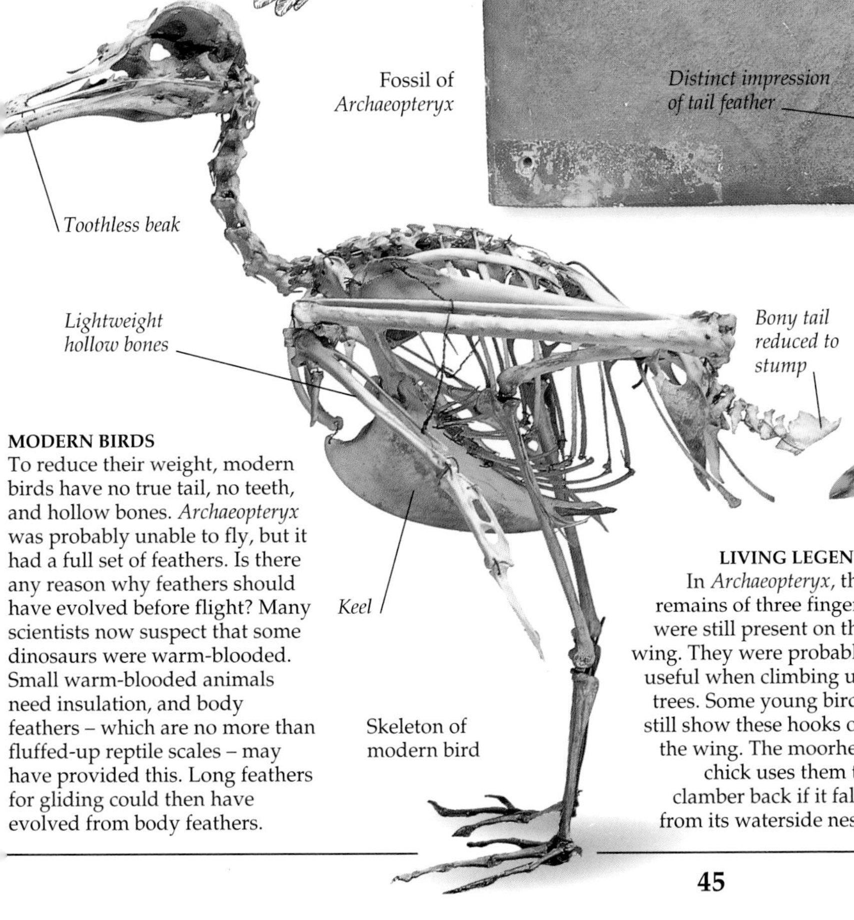

Distinct impression of tail feather

Toothless beak

Dinosaurlike skeleton of *Archaeopteryx*

Moorhen chick

Lightweight hollow bones

Bony tail reduced to stump

MODERN BIRDS

To reduce their weight, modern birds have no true tail, no teeth, and hollow bones. *Archaeopteryx* was probably unable to fly, but it had a full set of feathers. Is there any reason why feathers should have evolved before flight? Many scientists now suspect that some dinosaurs were warm-blooded. Small warm-blooded animals need insulation, and body feathers – which are no more than fluffed-up reptile scales – may have provided this. Long feathers for gliding could then have evolved from body feathers.

Keel

Skeleton of modern bird

LIVING LEGEND

In *Archaeopteryx*, the remains of three fingers were still present on the wing. They were probably useful when climbing up trees. Some young birds still show these hooks on the wing. The moorhen chick uses them to clamber back if it falls from its waterside nest.

Hooks on wing

45

Jumps and gaps

WHILE THERE ARE MANY INTERMEDIATE forms found in the fossil record (pp. 26 and 44), there are also many jumps and gaps. Evolutionists can now explain some of these, but not all. The most puzzling is the sudden appearance of many new and fairly complex animals in the Cambrian period (p. 26). This is still not understood, but scientists continue to investigate the problem. A second puzzle, the dramatic changes in fossils at the end of the Paleozoic era and the Mesozoic era, are now fairly well explained (below). A third problem is the lack of intermediates that bridge the gap between many groups, especially invertebrates. It seems that intermediate forms are relatively rare, perhaps because changes occur rapidly, and only in one small area of the world. This would mean that few intermediates become fossils. As a comparison, if a multistory parking garage was "fossilized" by a fall of volcanic ash, there would be plenty of cars fossilized on each level, but the chances of a car being fossilized while driving up from one level to the next would be relatively small.

THE CAMBRIAN EXPLOSION
This fossil from the Burgess shale in the Canadian Rocky Mountains belongs to the Cambrian period at the start of the Paleozoic era (below), when many new animals suddenly appeared. No definite ancestors have yet been identified.

CHANGING ERAS
As the early geologists noted (p. 16), the fossils from one geological period often differ from those of another. The differences among the three major eras (p. 60), which each include several geological periods, are even greater, as these three pieces of fossil-bearing rock show. The major differences between the fossils from successive eras are due to mass extinctions.

END OF THE MESOZOIC
Evidence suggests that the Mesozoic ended when a giant meteorite hit the Earth, forming a crater like this one in Arizona, but very much larger. Soil and rock dust were blasted into the air, blocking out sunlight and killing most plants. The lack of food would have killed off large animals such as dinosaurs. Mammals, then very small, were able to survive.

2 MESOZOIC
Triassic rock, containing ammonites, belongs to the Mesozoic era, the age of dinosaurs. Both dinosaurs and ammonites became extinct at the end of this era, 65 million years ago, when some 25 percent of species died out.

Rock containing fossilized sea shells and remains of trilobites

1 PALEOZOIC
This piece of rock is from the Silurian period in the Paleozoic era. This era ended 248 million years ago, when some 90 percent of species became extinct. The latest theory is that the amount of oxygen in the air fell sharply, suffocating most large, active animals.

LOST AND FOUND
The coelacanth is a fish that was thought to be extinct. All the known fossils were more than 200 million years old. Then, in 1938, a live coelacanth was fished out of the ocean. If the coelacanth could survive for 200 million years without leaving any fossils, it is not surprising that some steps in the evolution of life are not recorded.

HARD TO RECOGNIZE
Even when intermediate forms do become fossils, they may not be recognized as such. The dipper (below) dives for its food but looks like a land bird. Though it may evolve adaptations for underwater life, it has none yet. If dippers were extinct, no one would guess from their fossils how they had lived.

BURGESS BEAST
There is no reason to doubt that Cambrian animals, like this one from the Burgess shale, are descended from Precambrian life. All living things are united by the same basic chemistry and the same genetic code (p. 55).

LONG GONE
These soft-bodied creatures from Precambrian rock (right) lived just before the Cambrian, and are known as the Ediacara fauna. Most scientists think that they are unlikely ancestors for the Cambrian animals, but some disagree.

Fossil imprints of soft-bodied animals (left and below) from the Ediacara Hills in Australia

3 CENOZOIC
This rock (below right), bearing fossil fish, comes from the Tertiary period, part of the Cenozoic era. During the Cenozoic, which is still in progress, mammals and birds have taken over the many vacant slots left by the disappearance of the dinosaurs. After mass extinctions, some surviving species evolve into new forms that repopulate the Earth.

Fossil ammonite

Triassic rock

Tertiary rock

Fossil fish

Ladders and branches

ALL FOR PROGRESS
Ernst Haeckel (1834-1919) developed the idea of "evolution as progress" to its fullest extent. He believed that nature had been deliberately moving towards a final goal: human brings. The more that is discovered about what happened in the past, the less this idea makes sense.

In 19TH-CENTURY Europe and North America the Industrial Revolution was changing everyone's lives. Towns were growing rapidly, a network of railroads was spreading, and new factories were drawing thousands of workers from the countryside to the cities. Almost every aspect of social life was in a process of change. Most people, especially those in power, believed that all these changes amounted to "Progress," and that progress must be good. Evolution was a controversial idea for religious reasons, and linking it to progress made it far more acceptable. Darwin himself refrained from making this connection because he knew that the reality of evolution did not quite fit in with such ideas. For example, many types of bacteria have stayed small and simple for billions of years without "progressing" to become larger or more complex. This is also true of many other living things whose evolutionary history is more like a branching bush of diversification than a ladder of constant improvement. However, Darwin did not try to contradict two of his followers, Thomas Huxley and Ernst Haeckel, both of whom presented evolution in terms of progress. This rapidly became the popular view, and the idea is still widespread today.

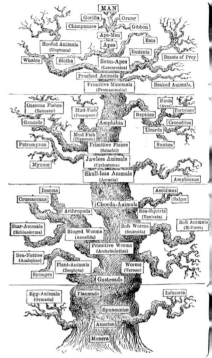

ECHOES OF THE PAST
As well as putting humans at the top, Haeckel's tree contains another of his theories: recapitulation. He believed that as an embryo developed it went through all the evolutionary stages of its ancestors. The five "ancestors" at the bottom of the tree trunk are based on the very early stages of development of an embryo.

GALLOPING UP
The evolution of the horse is often shown by a diagram such as this (left). Although the fossils of all these ancestors have indeed been found, this "ladder" gives a false picture. Evolution does not go in straight lines, and it is not always a steady march of progress from small-and-simple to large-and-complicated. A more realistic image is a densely branching bush (below). There have been dozens of species, most of which have died out, leaving just wild horses, donkeys, and zebras.

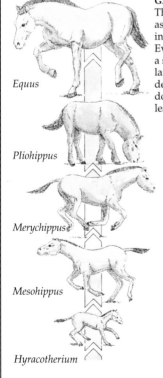

Equus

Pliohippus

Merychippus

Mesohippus

Hyracotherium

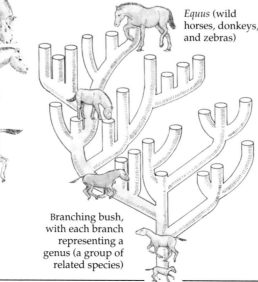

Equus (wild horses, donkeys, and zebras)

Branching bush, with each branch representing a genus (a group of related species)

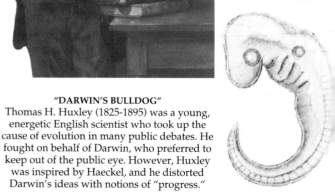

"DARWIN'S BULLDOG"
Thomas H. Huxley (1825-1895) was a young, energetic English scientist who took up the cause of evolution in many public debates. He fought on behalf of Darwin, who preferred to keep out of the public eye. However, Huxley was inspired by Haeckel, and he distorted Darwin's ideas with notions of "progress."

OUR MISSING TAIL (*below*)
The mistaken idea of recapitulation contains a grain of truth. Young embryos do resemble the embryos of related animals. For example, at about four weeks of age the human embryo (right) has a set of parallel grooves like those that lead to gill slits in fish. It also has a tail at this stage, which is later lost. The embryo does develop in a way which sometimes echoes its evolutionary past, but it does not reenact every step of its evolution as Haeckel suggested.

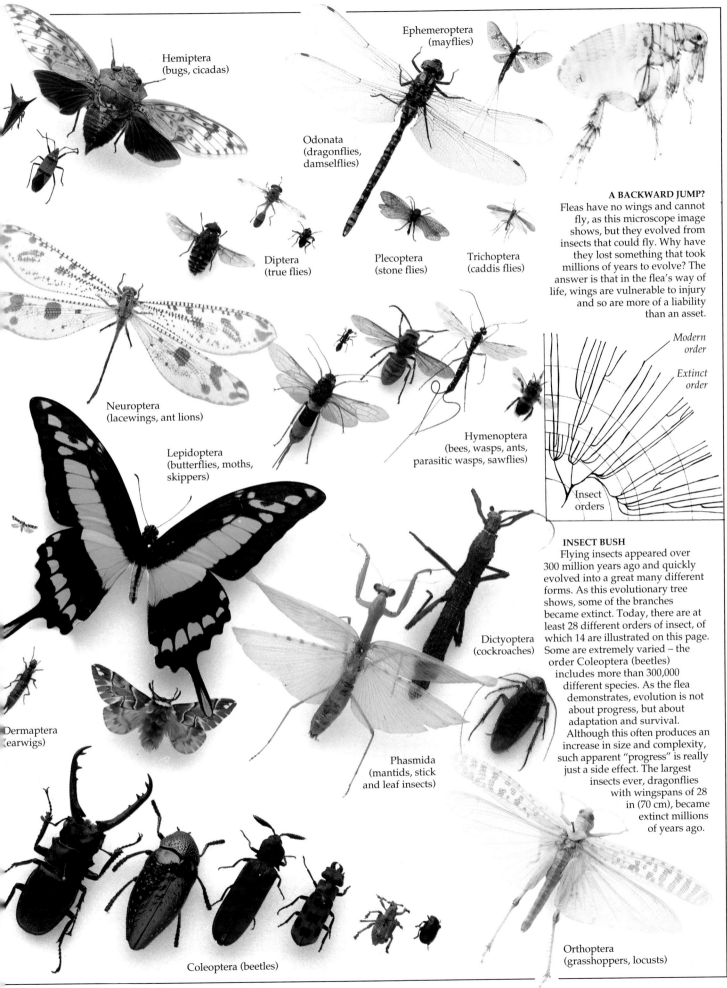

Hemiptera
(bugs, cicadas)

Ephemeroptera
(mayflies)

Odonata
(dragonflies,
damselflies)

Diptera
(true flies)

Plecoptera
(stone flies)

Trichoptera
(caddis flies)

A BACKWARD JUMP?
Fleas have no wings and cannot fly, as this microscope image shows, but they evolved from insects that could fly. Why have they lost something that took millions of years to evolve? The answer is that in the flea's way of life, wings are vulnerable to injury and so are more of a liability than an asset.

Modern order

Extinct order

Insect orders

Neuroptera
(lacewings, ant lions)

Lepidoptera
(butterflies, moths, skippers)

Hymenoptera
(bees, wasps, ants, parasitic wasps, sawflies)

INSECT BUSH
Flying insects appeared over 300 million years ago and quickly evolved into a great many different forms. As this evolutionary tree shows, some of the branches became extinct. Today, there are at least 28 different orders of insect, of which 14 are illustrated on this page. Some are extremely varied – the order Coleoptera (beetles) includes more than 300,000 different species. As the flea demonstrates, evolution is not about progress, but about adaptation and survival. Although this often produces an increase in size and complexity, such apparent "progress" is really just a side effect. The largest insects ever, dragonflies with wingspans of 28 in (70 cm), became extinct millions of years ago.

Dictyoptera
(cockroaches)

Dermaptera
(earwigs)

Phasmida
(mantids, stick and leaf insects)

Coleoptera (beetles)

Orthoptera
(grasshoppers, locusts)

Gregor Mendel

GREGOR MENDEL
The talented and intelligent son of a poor peasant, Mendel could continue his science studies only by entering the local monastery. Many of his fellow monks were enthusiastic scientists.

GREGOR MENDEL (1822-1884) was a monk and a physicist. Some of his fellow monks were crop breeders, and he began investigating heredity to help them to improve their crops. As a physicist, he looked for simple laws that could be expressed mathematically, and this happened to be a good way of approaching heredity. By an inspired guess, Mendel chose to study either/or characteristics, such as seed color in peas. Others scientists were looking at characteristics that appear to blend in the offspring, such as size. Though these are more common, they are far more difficult to study. Mendel's results, published in 1865, were not understood until 1900, when scientists made the same discoveries again. "Mendelism" was born, and in 1909 the word "gene" was coined for his hereditary particles (p. 52). At first Mendelism seemed to oppose Darwinism, because either/or characteristics would not create the small variations on which natural selection could work. In the 1920s it was realized that most characteristics are governed by dozens of genes, each with small effects that can add up to a large effect. The many genes controlling a characteristic such as size can provide small variations, but each gene behaves in exactly the same way as a gene for an either/or characteristic. The ideas of Mendelism clearly supported Darwin, and they were combined in a new theory – neo-Darwinism.

Variety 1 Self-fertilizing — yy Alleles in plants — yy Alleles in seeds — Seeds

Variety 2 Self-fertilizing — YY Alleles in plants — YY Alleles in seeds — Seeds

Variety 1 pollinated by variety 2 — Cross-pollination — Variety 2 pollinated by variety 1

Allele in egg — y Y Alleles in pollen — y Y — Allele in egg

Yy Yy Yy Yy Alleles in seeds — Yy Yy Yy Yy Seeds

Hybrid plant self-fertilizes (any hybrid seed from either plant will give the same result)

Yy Alleles in plant
Y or y Allele in egg
Y or y Allele in pollen
YY Yy Yy yy Alleles in seeds

MINIATURE TREES
Bonsai trees, like trees grown in harsh natural conditions, show how much external forces influence a characteristic such as size. The tree's genes (its "genotype") provide the raw material, but what happens to the tree helps to shape its actual form (the "phenotype"). To study heredity, it is important to look at characteristics that are not affected by external factors, or to keep the external factors exactly the same.

Bonsai yew, less than 1 ft (30 cm) tall

Tree stunted by severe pruning

A branch of normal yew, a tree that grows to a height of 82 ft (25 m)

Finding genes

Mendel worked with plant varieties (different types within a species). He crossed varieties that had distinct, contrasting characteristics, such as seed color. His results showed that heredity was not blending, but involved discrete units, now called genes.

CROSSING PEAS *(left)*
Mendel crossed a green-seeded variety of pea with a yellow one. (Pea flowers normally fertilize themselves, but they can be fertilized by hand with pollen from another plant.) All the seeds from the cross were yellow. These seeds were planted, and the plants were allowed to self-fertilize. They produced yellow and green peas, in a ratio of 3:1. This ratio reveals what is happening inside the plants. As Mendel realized, there must be hereditary particles (now called genes) that do not divide or blend. In this case, there is a single gene for seed color, but two different versions (or alleles) of the gene. One allele codes for yellow, the other for green. Each seed carries two alleles, and if they are of different types then the seed is yellow: the allele for yellow (called the dominant) masks the effect of the allele for green (called the recessive). Each seed receives one allele from the pollen and one allele from the egg.

Red ink

Blue ink

Red beads

Blue beads

Red and blue inks mixed to produce purple

Red and blue beads mixed to produce purple; each bead represents a single allele of one gene for flower color

BLENDING QUALITIES
If a plant variety with red flowers is crossed with another variety having blue flowers, the offspring usually have purple flowers. It appears that the effect is like that of mixing inks.

Inks cannot be separated

SEPARATING PARTICLES *(below)*
Heredity actually depends on particles called genes, but for most characteristics dozens of genes are involved, not just one as for the color of peas. Each gene has a small effect, but together they can add up to a large effect. The mixture of red and blue beads shows how the combined action of many genes can give a result that resembles blending inheritance, but this result is only superficial. By breeding from the purple-flowered hybrids, it is possible to get blue plants and red plants again. Like beads, the genes can be separated out again.

Unlike inks, differently colored beads can be separated out again

T.H. MORGAN (1866-1945)
Thomas Hunt Morgan, a scientist at Columbia University in New York City, began his work on fruit flies in 1907. His work helped lead to the realization that most characteristics are controlled by many genes.

BRED IN BOTTLES
Fruit flies (*Drosophila*) are far easier to study than plants. They can be kept in bottles, they breed quickly, and they often undergo spontaneous changes (called mutations) in their genes. Through his work on these flies, Morgan managed to locate each gene at a specific site, or "locus," on a chromosome. Chromosomes are situated in the nucleus, at the centre of every cell.

Tiny mutant fruit fly

Normal fly

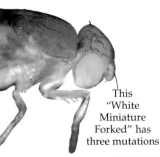

This "White Miniature Forked" has three mutations

Normal fly

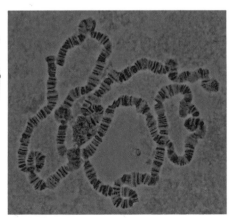

SEEING GENES
Fruit flies offer an added bonus to geneticists – they have giant chromosomes in their salivary glands, and because of their size these can be studied more easily than normal chromosomes. Each band on the chromosomes corresponds to an individual gene site, or "locus." Genes are now known to consist of DNA (p. 52).

Solving the DNA puzzle

Base pair

Base pair

Strand of helix

Strand of helix

DOUBLE HELIX
This illustration shows the different base pairs that make up the rungs of the DNA molecule. Each base will only fit with one other base.

X-RAY VISION
Rosalind Franklin (1921-1958) studied crystals of DNA using X-ray diffraction. The way in which the crystals scatter the X-rays reveals the structure and chemistry of the molecules in the crystal. Rosalind Franklin's images confirmed earlier theories about DNA, that its molecule is indeed a double helix.

By the 1920s, it was clear that the chromosomes (p. 51) carry the genes. Chromosomes were found to contain both deoxyribonucleic acid (DNA) and protein, and no one knew which was the hereditary material. James Watson (b. 1928) and Francis Crick (b. 1916) guessed that it was DNA; they hoped that, by working out its structure, they could understand heredity. They had seen X-ray images of DNA, and they knew the shape and chemistry of its various components. Using all this information, they tried to work out the structure by building models. Success came in 1953 and, as they had hoped, the structure revealed how heredity worked. The molecule is like a ladder twisted into a helix. The rungs of the ladder are made up of chemical compounds called bases, two per rung (called a base pair). There are four different types of base available (adenine, thymine, cytosine, and guanine). The breakthrough for Watson and Crick was the realization that adenine could pair only with thymine, while guanine could pair only with cytosine. They saw that this would enable DNA to divide and yet produce perfect copies of itself, and that the order of the bases along the molecule could contain the genetic information.

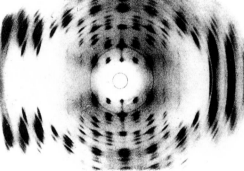

MAPPING MOLECULES
Rosalind Franklin's X-ray diffraction pictures also revealed that the sugar and phosphate units of DNA were on the outside of the helix. This was vital information for Watson and Crick.

STRANDS OF LIFE
In order to copy itself, the DNA molecule divides. The two strands of the helix come apart, little by little, as the base pairs separate. Then new bases pair on to the existing ones on each strand. The fact that each base can only pair with one other base ensures that each half of the original helix becomes an exact copy of the complete original. This is how the hereditary information is passed on from one generation to the next. Occasionally, however, a mistake can occur in the copying, and this results in a genetic mutation (p. 32). Mutations can provide a valuable source of raw material for evolution.

Original DNA molecule

Base

Copies forming

WINNING MODEL *(left)*
This is part of the original model of the DNA molecule, made by James Watson (left) and Francis Crick (right) in 1953. The base pairs, or rungs, are arranged along the strands of the DNA molecule in what seems like a random order. In fact, the order of the bases is full of information and can be translated according to the "genetic code."

Sugar molecule

Phosphate molecule

Sugar molecule

Base

Base

Linked molecules forming one strand of DNA helix

Second strand of helix

THE GENETIC CODE

This modern model of the DNA double helix shows that the two long strands forming the backbones of the helix are made of identical sugar and phosphate molecules. Only the bases vary. Starting at a particular place on the helix, every group of three bases acts as a "codon" and translates into a particular amino acid. The long string of amino acids that is produced by reading in this way makes up a protein strand. Each gene consists of thousands of bases and codes for one strand of one protein. These proteins include thousands of different enzymes, which control all the chemical reactions taking place in the body. Such reactions produce growth, movement, behavior, digestion, and all other life processes. By issuing its "commands" in the form of enzymes and other proteins, DNA controls every aspect of living things.

Acorns

TOXIC ACORNS

A difference in their DNA makes European red squirrels less well fed than North American gray squirrels. Gray squirrels have an enzyme that breaks down toxins in acorns, so they can feast on acorns in winter. Red squirrels lack the DNA for this enzyme and cannot benefit as much from acorns. They have almost died out in the UK, largely due to competition from introduced gray squirrels.

INHERITED PATTERN

The coat pattern of the Himalayan rabbit is due to a gene mutation. This causes the enzyme that produces the dark pigment, melanin, to break down when it is warm. The enzyme works only in the cooler parts of the body, such as ears and paws. This means that only these parts have any melanin.

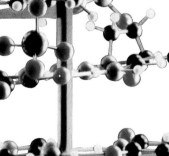

Himalayan rabbit

Molecular evidence

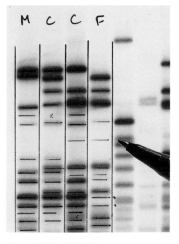

DNA FINGERPRINTS
Comparing DNA is a useful way of finding out how closely living things are related. Here DNA from two children (C and C) is being compared with DNA from each of their parents (M and F). This version of the method is called "DNA fingerprinting." It can be used to identify the father of a child, for example. DNA fingerprints can also be taken from blood stains, and these are sometimes used to help in the identification of criminals.

SINCE THE WORK OF Watson and Crick (p. 52), scientists have continued to study DNA. They have found that DNA itself, and the proteins it produces, contain vital evidence about evolution. If two new species evolve from a common ancestor, their DNA, and thus their protein molecules, slowly begin to change and build up differences. The number of differences is proportional to the time since they separated. This discovery was made during the 1960s and a possible explanation was proposed by a Japanese scientist, Motoo Kimura. He suggested that many mutations (p. 32) have neither good nor bad effects. He called these "neutral mutations." Such a mutation could change one of the amino acids in a protein molecule (p. 53) without affecting how the protein does its job in the body. Kimura's theory is still disputed, but the fact that mutations build up at a regular rate is not in doubt. It is as if the molecules inside the body carry a steadily ticking clock that creates a record of the past. This can be used to check the accuracy of evolutionary trees worked out from fossils or from comparisons of the structure of living things. This independent source of evidence largely confirms the evolutionary trees already worked out, indicating that scientific ideas about evolution are correct.

DEEP FROZEN
The bodies of now-extinct mammoths are sometimes found in the icy ground of Siberia. These remains still contain DNA, although it is partially broken down. This ancient DNA can be compared with that of the mammoth's relative, the elephant.

Family tree of elephants and their close relatives

- African elephant
- Asian elephant
- Mammoth (extinct)
- Mastodon (extinct)
- Steller's sea cow (extinct)
- Dugong
- West Indian manatee
- Brazilian manatee
- West African manatee
- Hyrax
- Aardvark
- Other mammals

Time scale (millions of years ago)
60   40   20   0

PROTEINS FROM THE PAST
One simple way of comparing proteins is to use the immune system. This is the system that animals have for defense against disease. It reacts to foreign substances very specifically, so if an animal such as a rabbit has been "vaccinated" with proteins from an elephant, its immune system will also react to proteins from a relative of the elephant, for instance a mammoth, but not as strongly. The closer the relationship, the stronger the reaction. The family tree (left) for elephants and their close relatives was worked out in this way.

Preserved mammoth from Siberia

A   B   C

Hermit crabs

Alaskan king crab

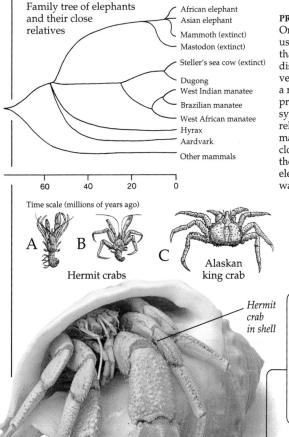

Hermit crab in shell

- Hermit crab
- Hermit crab
- Hermit crab
- Hermit crab
- A
- Hermit crab
- Hermit crab
- B
- C
- Hermit crab
- Hermit crab
- Hermit crab

TESTING A THEORY
Hermit crabs are small and depend on the shells of mollusks for their homes. Because of their habit of living in spiral shells, the hindpart of the body, the abdomen, is curved to one side. Alaskan king crabs are large and never live in mollusk shells, but zoologists suspected that they had evolved from hermit crabs because their abdomens are slightly assymmetrical, like those of hermit crabs. When DNA comparisons became possible, zoologists saw a way of testing this theory. They extracted DNA from many different species of hermit crab and from Alaskan king crabs. Comparisons showed that king crabs are indeed very closely related to the hermit crabs (left). As with the mammoths, elephants, and sea cow (manatees), the DNA confirmed what was already thought on the basis of more traditional evidence.

E

F

G

H

Insect

Flowering plant

SAY IT WITH FLAGS

Semaphore, like most codes, is arbitrary. There is no reason why a flag held out with the left hand should mean "F," but everyone using the code knows that it does. In the same way, the genetic code, by which DNA is translated into protein, is arbitrary. The three bases on DNA, cytosine-cytosine-guanine (in that order), code for the amino acid proline in a protein strand. Yet there is no reason why they should code for proline rather than another amino acid.

Mammal

Scorpion

Fungus

Mollusk

ONE CODE FOR ALL

A very powerful piece of evidence for evolution is the fact that all living things – from insects to fungi, from humans to viruses – share the same genetic code (p. 53). If there had been more than one life form originally, why should they all have adopted this same code, where each codon (three DNA bases) has acquired a fixed but entirely arbitrary meaning? If, on the other hand, all life is descended from one ancestor, this makes perfect sense. Once the code was established, it would be very difficult for any changes in the code to evolve, since these would undermine the whole system, making protein production impossible. Presumably, the code evolved at a very early stage in the development of life. Fossil evidence suggests that the earliest forms were bacteria (p. 56), so it seems likely that they "invented" the genetic code now shared by all living things.

Sponge

The origin of life

HOW DID LIFE BEGIN? Could it have originated from nonliving matter by ordinary chemical processes? The earliest fossils are bacterial cells, 3,800 million years old. Before that there is no solid evidence about the evolution of life, so scientists have to approach these questions in other ways. One approach is to try to recreate the conditions found on the early Earth. Such experiments were first tried during the 1950s and, to most people's surprise, they readily produced the sort of complex chemicals that are found only in living things. These include the building blocks of proteins, DNA and RNA (a molecule similar to DNA that is involved in protein production). If complex molecules such as these could have arisen spontaneously billions of years ago, why do they not still do so today? The answer is that conditions now are quite different. Most importantly, there is oxygen in the air, while there was almost none in the Earth's atmosphere then. Once complex chemicals had formed on the early Earth, several important steps would have been required before they became genuine living things. Some scientists believe that the first major step was the formation of an RNA molecule that could make exact copies of itself. Recently, small molecules of this kind have been made in the laboratory. A second major step was the development of a relationship between RNA and proteins and the establishment of a genetic code (p. 55).

ENERGY INPUT
The chemicals found in living things are far more complex than those found in rocks or sea or air. To create complex molecules from simple ones, energy is required. One likely source of this energy on the early Earth was lightning.

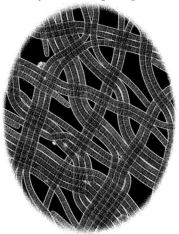

SELF-SUFFICIENCY BEGINS
The first bacteria must have lived by feeding on the complex chemicals still being produced, but in time they ate more than was being formed. When the supply ran short, many bacteria must have died out, but others, that could make their own food, evolved. These included the cyanobacteria, or blue-green algae (left).

THE OXYGEN REVOLUTION
Some bacteria use energy from the Sun to make their own food, as plants do, and in the process they release oxygen gas. When the first of these bacteria evolved, more then 2,500 million years ago, they began to produce oxygen, which slowly built up in the air. The oxygen combined with iron in the rocks to produce bands of ironstone (right) at this time. Oxygen changed the conditions on Earth so much that many creatures became extinct. In time, oxygen in the air also allowed new, larger, and more active animals to evolve. Such active life forms would have been impossible without oxygen.

STEPS TO LIFE
Almost all living things today are composed of cells. It is hard to say exactly when living things became cellular. Some theorists suggest that the earliest life forms were "naked" RNA molecules, not surrounded by any membrane. Others believe that a membrane of some sort came first, before RNA. They point out that certain large molecules spontaneously form droplets, inside which other molecules could accumulate.

SEALED UNIT
A cell is rather like a submarine. The membrane of the cell acts like the hull, creating a sealed unit in which the internal conditions can be closely controlled. Only certain substances are allowed to pass in or out

In this apparatus, a spark of
electrical discharge makes simple
gases combine to produce complex
molecules such as amino acids
(found in proteins) and bases
(found in DNA and RNA).

Electrical supply

Electrode

*Tube through
which gases
circulate*

Electrode

The dawn of life?

In the early 1950s, an American
chemist, Stanley Miller, devised
experiments to test ideas about
the origin of life. He excluded all
oxygen from his apparatus and
filled it with methane,
ammonia, hydrogen, and
water vapor to simulate
the atmosphere of the
ancient Earth. Miller
provided an electrical
spark to mimic the flashes
of lightning that could
have provided a source
of energy. At the end
of the experiment, his
apparatus contained
complex molecules –
the kinds of molecules
found only in living
things. As yet, only
one experimenter has
managed to persuade
these building blocks to
join up spontaneously into
longer molecules, such as
proteins and DNA or RNA –
the next crucial step in
the evolution of life.

EDUCATED GUESSES
Stanley Miller, seen here at work
in his laboratory, proposed that
gases given off by volcanoes
would have helped create the
atmosphere of the ancient Earth.
Other scientists agree with this,
but some have disagreed about
the exact gases present. They
know that little oxygen was
present and that there was
probably water vapor in the air,
but little else is certain. However,
on the basis of educated guesses,
several likely combinations of
gases have been tried. Almost all
of them have been found to
produce the complex chemicals
typical of living things.

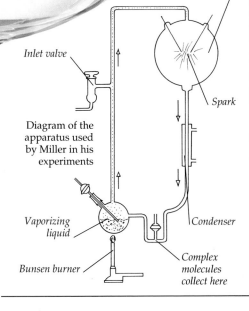

*Gas-filled
reaction
chamber*

Inlet valve

Spark

Diagram of the
apparatus used
by Miller in his
experiments

*Vaporizing
liquid*

Condenser

Bunsen burner

*Complex
molecules
collect here*

Science and belief

APE OR ANGEL?
A 19th-century French cartoon shows Darwin in apelike form, bursting through the hoops of credulity and ignorance held by the French physician and philosopher Maximilien Littré (1801-1881), a supporter of Darwin. The evidence that humans arose from apelike ancestors by evolution is very strong (p. 63), but this idea troubles many people. Alfred Wallace (p. 36) solved his dilemma between science and belief by proposing that, while human beings had indeed evolved, the human spirit came from some supernatural source.

MANY DIFFERENT CULTURES have traditional beliefs about how the living world was made (p. 6). These beliefs are not usually open to question or change. Scientific ideas about the history of life are different: the details of the story are continually changing because scientists work by looking for new evidence, by questioning existing theories and trying to develop better theories. In time, some theories become well established, and their basic points are accepted as fact simply because the evidence in their favor is overwhelming. The idea that the Earth goes around the Sun is one such theory. The idea that evolution has occurred is another. There may still be arguments over the details of how evolution occurred, but the fact that it did occur is not in doubt among most scientists.

One way of testing theories is to use them to make predictions and then to check those predictions. Because evolution proceeds so slowly, it is more difficult to test in this way than other scientific theories. (For the same reason, we do not normally notice evolution in action around us, even though it is continuing all the time.) Occasionally, however, evolutionary theories can be tested in the wild. A theory about how social insects evolved was used to make a prediction about evolution in mammals, and this was later confirmed by discoveries about the naked mole rat. Theories about natural selection were tested by observing the effects of cleaner air on the peppered moth.

SCIENCE AND THE PRESS
Stephen Jay Gould (b. 1942) is among the scientists who are continually testing and questioning the details of evolution theory. Sadly, newspapers often fail to understand this scientific process and assume that the whole idea of evolution is in doubt. They then report the scientific debates under dramatic and misleading headlines, such as the one below.

Darwin Wrong Scientist Claims
by our Science Correspondent

CLEANER AIR, PALER MOTHS
A dark form of the peppered moth replaced the paler form in industrial areas of England from the 1850s onward. Scientists suspected that this was a result of pollution, reducing the camouflage of the pale moths (p. 36). Natural selection by moth-eating birds was thought to be at work. When, in the 1970s, laws were passed to reduce pollution, an unintentional "experiment" took place, allowing scientists to check their theory about why the darker form had taken over. In the next few years the air became cleaner. As predicted, the numbers of dark moths did fall, while the paler ones increased.

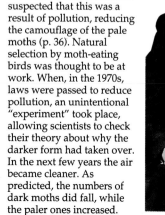

ON THE WRONG TRACK?
Could scientists be totally mistaken about evolution? This claim is sometimes made by opponents of the theory. However, in science, mistaken ideas do not survive for long, because theories are tested against experimental evidence. The case of Soviet geneticist Trofim Lysenko (1898-1976) proved this point. He favored Lamarckian ideas (p. 13), since they agreed with communist ideology, and he rose to power under Stalin. Lysenko banished Mendelian geneticists (p. 50), and dominated Soviet genetics for many years. Eventually, however, the evidence against Lamarckian inheritance was so strong that ideology had to give way to science. Lysenko was discredited and forced to resign.

Puzzle and prediction

Social insects, such as bees, wasps, and ants, live in colonies in which a single female produces all the offspring while the other members of the colony carry out duties of protection and feeding. How such social insects could have evolved has long been a puzzle. In the 1970s, the American zoologist Richard Alexander proposed an answer. He suggested that an insect species that cares for its young might evolve into a social insect as a direct result of living in a "fortress of food" – a well-defended nest to which food can be imported, or in which food is already available. He also made the bold prediction that a social mammal could evolve to live like these insects.

WASP NEST

Wasps are social insects, like bees and termites. Each colony builds a complex nest, and at the center of this nest, one female can remain safe and well fed. She produces all the young. The other wasps defend the colony or go out to collect food. Even if they are killed, their genes are passed on to the next generation, because the queen shares those genes. Until 1976, this odd way of life was known only among insects.

Naked mole rat hills formed during tunnelling

THE UNLIKELY MAMMAL

Alexander suggested that a mammal with a social life like a bee could have evolved. He predicted that if it did so, it would probably live in a place with a long dry season, where some plants have huge tubers. The mammal would be a burrower that could build its underground colony – its "fortress of food" – around these tubers. Several years later, to the amazement of scientists, South African zoologist Jennifer Jarvis demonstrated that the naked mole rat, an East African mammal, lives precisely as Richard Alexander had predicted.

DIGGING BLINDLY

Like a worker wasp, the naked mole rat worker spends its time defending the colony, bringing food to the young, or tunnelling through the earth to find the tubers on which the colony feeds. While digging, it can close its mouth behind its front teeth, to avoid swallowing earth. It is almost blind, rarely venturing into daylight.

Worker gathering food

Naked mole rat queen in burrow

UNDERGROUND QUEEN

The queen is the only mole rat in the colony to produce offspring. She keeps the other females infertile by her dominant behavior. She remains in the safety of the deepest part of the burrow (above) and is vigorously protected by the workers. In the nest chamber she suckles the young (right) until they are old enough to be fed on tubers by the workers.

Baby naked mole rats suckle at the queen's teats

DISPOSABLE WORKER

The workers live and die without producing any young. When the colony is under attack by a snake, workers may sacrifice their own lives in order to defend the colony, just as worker bees do.

Naked mole rat worker

The queen is larger than the workers

History of life

THE SCIENTIFIC STUDY of rocks, fossils, and living things can be used to build a picture of what happened in the past. Hundreds of scientists, working in different parts of the world, have helped build this picture. The details change as new evidence is constantly being found, and there are differences of opinion among scientists about some of the specific points. However, there is broad agreement on the major events, the general course of evolution, and the time scale.

BEFORE LIFE
Meteorites were formed at the same time as the Earth (p. 29). The Earth's crust solidified 4,500 million years ago, but for millions of years the Earth was empty of life. Although the early steps in the origin of life can only be guessed at (p. 56), the first fossils are of bacteria, some 3,800 million years old.

BACTERIAL FOSSILS
Bacteria evolved into many types with different ways of obtaining their food. Some cyanobacteria (p. 56) form colonies that are large enough to be seen without the aid of a microscope.

GETTING LARGER
Only at the end of the Precambrian do a few multicellular animals appear in the fossil record. Most belong to the Ediacara fauna (p. 47).

CAMBRIAN EXPLOSION
In the Cambrian, large numbers of multicellular animals suddenly appear in the fossil record (p. 26).

BURGESS SHALE
Cambrian rocks reveal many different groups of invertebrate animals.

CONTINENTAL DRIFT
Throughout the history of life, the continents have moved about the globe. Climates have changed, and the sea level has risen and fallen many times.

Dry land

Shallow sea

SIMPLE SURVIVORS
In this fossil colony of bryozoans, each opening contained a single tiny animal. Still found today, bryozoans have shown little change for millions of years, like many other simple creatures.

NAUTILOID
Long-shelled nautiloids such as *Orthoceras* (p. 27) were among the invertebrate animals that inhabited the seas of the Ordovician period.

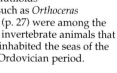

SILURIAN SEAS
Primitive crustaceans known as trilobites were abundant and widespread during the Ordovician and Silurian periods. Fossils of feeding tracks show that they lived on the sea floor. They later became extinct, as did the giant sea scorpions, large armoured animals up to 6 ft (2 m) long, with huge pincers.

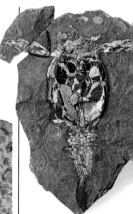

ARMORED FISH
The early fish were covered in plates of bony armor, probably as a defense against the giant sea scorpions abundant at that time.

AGE OF FISH
During the Devonian, the Earth looked like this. The climate was very hot, and sea levels fell. The heat and drought affected the course of evolution. The drying up of rivers and pools favored the development of lungs in several groups of fish (p. 42), one of which later evolved into the amphibians. In other fish, the lungs evolved into a swim bladder.

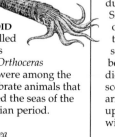

PRECAMBRIAN	CAMBRIAN PERIOD	ORDOVICIAN PERIOD	SILURIAN PERIOD	DEVONIAN PERIOD
PALEOZOIC ERA				

TIME SPAN
Most of the history of life
is taken up by simple
single-celled animals,
largely bacteria. They
were the only living
things for almost
3,000 million years.
Compared with this, the
extinction of the dinosaurs
at the end of the Mesozoic,
65 million years ago, seems
like a fairly recent event,
as does the emergence of
modern humans, just
100,000 years ago.

Geological time scale

MESOZOIC

PALAEOZOIC

| 3,500 MYA | 2,000 MYA | **PRECAMBRIAN** |

4,500
**MILLION
YEARS AGO
(MYA)**

*Bacteria first
appear*

*Oxygen builds
up in atmosphere*

*First fossils of
multicellular animals*

CENOZOIC

FOSSIL FERN
Plants, like animals,
evolved from bacterial
ancestors, probably during
the late Precambrian. The
simplest plants were one-
celled algae. From these
evolved seaweeds, mosses,
ferns, trees, and all other
plants, past and present.

Procynosuchus,
a mammal-like
reptile from the
late Permian

AGE OF REPTILES
During the Jurassic, the dinosaurs expanded
and diverged, to become the dominant
land animals of the Cretaceous
period. *Tyrannosaurus* (right),
a large meat-eating dinosaur,
did not emerge until the end
of this long reptile reign.

VEGETARIAN DINOSAUR
Iguanodon (below), a
plant-eating dinosaur,
was very common in the
mid-Cretaceous but then
died out. Throughout
this period, many new
species of dinosaur
evolved, while others
became extinct.

RISE OF THE REPTILES
During the Permian, the
earliest mammal-like
reptiles had emerged
and become very
widespread and
abundant. Many died
out at the end of the
Permian, along with
many of the amphibians.
This cleared the way for
a new phase of reptile
evolution. More
advanced mammal-like
reptiles appeared and
flourished during the
Triassic, along with the
ancestors of dinosaurs.

EARLY BIRD
The fossil remains of
Archaeopteryx suggest
that birds had begun to
evolve from dinosaurs
during the Jurassic.

LIFE ON LAND
Life existed only in
the sea until the early
Devonian. By the
Carboniferous, fish had
followed plants and insects
on to the land. Some had
evolved into amphibians
that lived in huge forests of
giant horsetails and ferns.

**STRANGE
FOSSIL**
The arrow-
headed amphibian
Diplocaulus lived during
the Permian. The legs of
this fossil are missing.

SUPER-CONTINENT
At the end of the Permian,
more than 90 percent of all
species died out, the largest
mass extinction (p. 46) of
all time. During the
Permian, all the continents
collided to form one super-
continent, called Pangea.

**SPIRAL
SURVIVORS**
By the Triassic, most
nautiloids had tightly coiled
shells. The more specialized
ammonites became extinct at
the end of the Cretaceous, but
some nautiloids survived.

FOSSIL FROG
After the Permian period,
amphibians were never
as widespread or diverse
again, but they left many
successors mostly small
animals such as frogs,
salamanders, and newts.

CHANGING WORLD
By the end of the
Cretaceous, the single
super-continent had split
up, and the continents
were moving apart
toward their present
positions. At the end of
this era there was a mass
extinction in which all the
dinosaurs and many other
animal species died out.

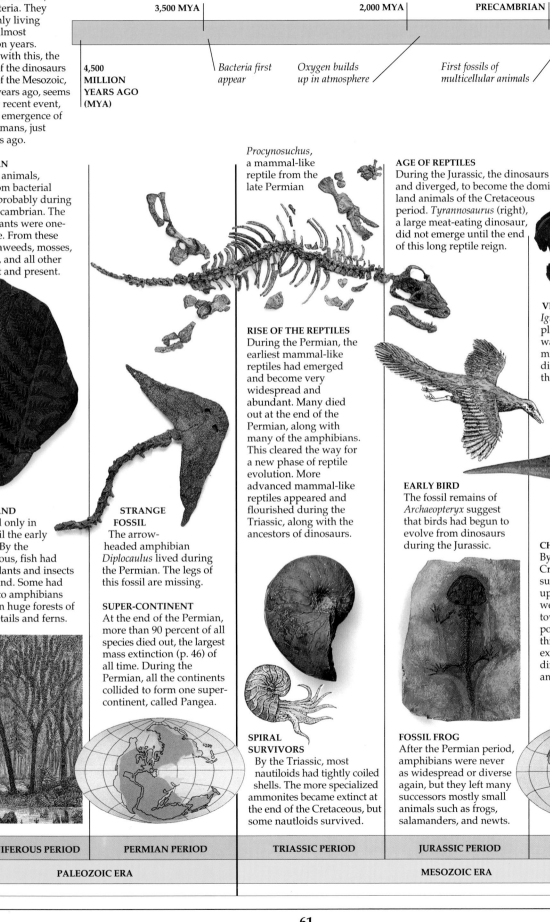

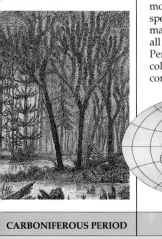

CARBONIFEROUS PERIOD	**PERMIAN PERIOD**	**TRIASSIC PERIOD**	**JURASSIC PERIOD**	**CRETACEOUS PERIOD**
PALEOZOIC ERA		**MESOZOIC ERA**		

Up to the present

FOR THE PAST 65 MILLION YEARS, mammals have been the dominant land animals. Their ancestors were small nocturnal creatures that evolved 200 million years ago from the mammal-like reptiles. During the age of the dinosaurs, they remained small and unobtrusive but, in the vacuum left by the extinction of the dinosaurs, mammals evolved rapidly, growing larger and far more diverse. So too did the birds, but their bones are fragile and do not fossilize easily, so there are relatively few birds in the fossil record.

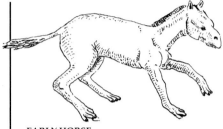

EARLY HORSE
Hyracotherium is the earliest horselike fossil, from 55 million years ago. The fact that evolution is not a steady march of progress is well illustrated by the horse (p. 48) and by mammal evolution in general. However, there has been an increase in speed, intelligence, or size, in some mammal lines.

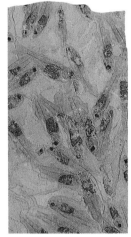

FISH AND PLANTS
It is not only the dominant animals (such as mammals) that continue to evolve, although this is the part of the story that attracts most interest. During the Cenozoic, there has been change among fish (above) and plants (left), as well as other living things.

SEAL FORERUNNER
Many of the early mammals were very much like dogs in shape and build. They gradually evolved into more specialized forms, such as seals, deer, and horses.

MIGHTY MASTODON
This vertebra (below) is from a mastodon (p. 14), an elephant-like animal that browsed on trees. The American mastodon survived into the Quaternary period and only died out about 10,000 years ago. Like many other large mammals that died out at this time, it may have fallen victim to human hunters.

ICE AGE BEAR
This cave bear skull is about 20,000 years old. These large bears lived during the last Ice Age and survived the extreme cold of winter by hibernating in caves. Mammals from the Quaternary period were more like present-day mammals than were those of the Teritiary, but many were far larger than their modern relatives.

END OF THE LINE
The extinct *Paleotherium* is known from this jaw and other fossils. It was a tapirlike animal.

EVOLUTIONARY ISLANDS
The separation of the continents affected mammal evolution greatly, with distinctive groups developing in isolated continents.

ALMOST AN ELEPHANT
The fossil known as *Phiomia* is part of the group that later gave rise to elephants, mammoths, and mastodons.

SABRE-TOOTH
Large tigerlike predators with massive stabbing teeth evolved to prey on slow-moving, thick-skinned creatures such as mammoths.

ANCIENT APE
Proconsul was an early ape that lived about 20 million years ago. Apes evolved from monkeys. They were very diverse 20 million years ago, but many died out as the Earth's climate grew drier and the forests shrank.

ADVANCED LEAF
These leaves, which are about 20 million years old, are from a flowering plant, the most recent plant form to evolve. These only appeared during the Cretaceous. Until then the dominant plants were the conifers and cycads.

Fossil Miocene leaves

VANISHED BIRD
Moas, the giant birds of New Zealand (p. 25), show what might have happened in a world without mammals – birds could have become dominant. Early in the Tertiary period, when mammals were still all fairly small, birds did in fact dominate. Huge flightless predatory birds evolved and preyed on mammals.

TERTIARY PERIOD

CENOZOIC ERA

Artist's impression
of Glyptodon

ARMORED ANIMAL
The glyptodon, one of South America's many unique mammal species, is now extinct. After a long interval as an island, South America was reunited with North America by a fall in sea level. Competition, or predation, by invaders from the north forced many South American mammals into extinction.

Bony plates of
Glyptodon

CLEVER NEANDERTHALS
The skull of Neanderthals suggests a brain at least as large as that of modern humans. The image of Neanderthals as dim and brutish is based on a mistaken 19th-century study of a skeleton. However, they were very strong and stocky and seem to have been well suited to the Ice Age climate.

THE MODERN WORLD
By the Quaternary, the continents had almost reached their present positions. Their slow movement around the globe is still continuing, however, and this produces earthquakes in some places, such as California. Ice ages – four in all – have been an important factor in evolution during the Quaternary period, cooling the climate all over the world.

Ice

LEAF EATER
Megatherium, the giant ground sloth of South America, probably fed by sitting on its haunches and pulling down tree branches or whole trees to eat the leaves.

QUATERNARY PERIOD

CENOZOIC ERA

Human evolution

The fossil record gives a clear picture of how upright-walking, large-brained creatures called hominids evolved from an apelike ancestor. Many skulls of the intermediate stages have been found, as well as some almost complete skeletons. These show that upright walking was the first stage and that the brain gradually increased in size after that. Molecular evidence (p. 54) suggests that the hominid and ape lines separated about 5 million years ago. Unfortunately, there are few fossil-bearing rocks of this age in Africa, where they evolved, and the earliest hominid fossils are from about 3.5 million years ago. These hominids already walked upright. The first fossils that are physically identical to modern humans date from 40,000 years ago.

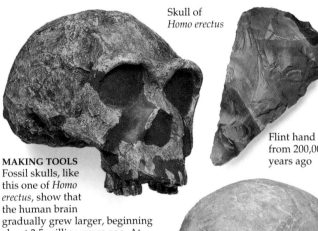

Skull of
Homo erectus

Flint hand axe
from 200,000
years ago

MAKING TOOLS
Fossil skulls, like this one of *Homo erectus*, show that the human brain gradually grew larger, beginning about 2.5 million years ago. At the same time, the ridges above the eyes became smaller, and the face and jaw began to jut out less. Increasing intelligence and the ability to make better tools apparently went together. The earliest stone tools, made in Africa about 2.5 million years ago, were simpler than the hand ax shown here.

Modern
human skull

BIGGER BRAINS
Increasing intelligence undoubtedly contributed to the survival of early hominids. For example, *Homo erectus* cooperated to hunt large animals, and this would have required language and intelligence. But the very great intelligence and creativity of modern humans seem to go beyond what might have aided survival in the wild. It is difficult to see musical gifts or mathematical abilities as a result of natural selection. Some human behavior, good and bad, actually runs contrary to natural selection.

Mozart, the musical child prodigy

Index

Acknowledgments

**Dorling Kindersley would like
to thank:**
Jeremy Adams, John Cooper and Gerald
Legg at the Booth Museum, Hove; Solene
Morris at Downe House; Nick Arnold,
Ian Bishop, David Carter, Sandra
Chapman, Paul Clark, Andy Currant,
Paul Hillyard, Jerry Hooker, Robert
Kruszynski, David Lewis, Tim
Parmenter, Alison Paul, David Reid, Lee
Rogers and Sally Young at the Natural
History Museum; Denise Blagden; Tom
Kemp, Philip Powell, Monica Price and
Derek Siveter at the Oxford University
Museum; and Jack Challoner, for all their
advice and help with the provision of
objects for photography; Margaret Brown
of the Medical Research Council,
Cambridge; Chris Faulkes of the Institute
of Zoology, London; and Jim Hamill at
the British Museum (Ethnographic), for
their help; Sarah Ashun, Jonathan
Buckley, Jane Burton, Peter Chadwick,
Philip Dowell, Andreas von Einsiedel,
Frank Greenaway, Derek Hall, Colin

Keates, Dave King, Karl Shone and Jerry
Young for photography; Deborah Rhodes
for page make-up.

DTP Manager Joanna Figg-Latham
Illustrations Stephen Bull and Frazer May
Index Jane Parker

Publisher's note No animal has been
injured or in any way harmed during the
preparation of this book.

Picture credits

t=top b=bottom c=center l=left r=right

American Philosophical Society,
Philadelphia 15bl.
Ancient Art and Architecture Collection
8br; 16br.
Bettmann Archive 50bl; 57bl.
Bridgeman Art Library 20bl.
Department of Palaeontology, Royal
Belgian Institute of Natural Sciences,
Brussels 19tr.

William Sturgis Bigelow Collection,
Museum of Fine Arts, Boston 6tr.
British Library 7bl; 7bc.
British Museum 16bl.
Neil Bromhall 59cr; 59cl.
Brown Brothers 41br.
By permission of the Syndics of
Cambridge University Library 30cl.
Camera Press 52bl; 58tr.
Bruce Coleman /Stephen Bord 11tr; 35tl;
/Pekka Hallor 39br; 43br; /Konrad
Wothe 47cr; /Hans Rheinard 53br.
Mary Evans Picture Library 9bl; 10tl;
13br; 19cl; 25bc; 42-3c; 48cr; 56br; 61bl.
Chris Faulkes 59tr.
Werner Foreman Archive 7tl.
Giraudon 40tl.
Michael Holford 6bc; 30bl.
Hulton Deutsche Collection Ltd 13tr;
13cr; 17cr; 21cl; 28tl; 36bc; 43tr; 54cr.
Illustrated London News Picture
Library 30cr.
Mansell Collection 12tl; 14tl; 17tl; 19bl;
20cl; 21cr; 29tl; 33cl; 34tr; 36tl; 41cl;
42cl; 63br.

Professor Rory Mortimore, University of
Brighton 11cr.
MRC Laboratory of Molecular Biology 53l.
Natural History Museum Picture Library
12cr; 18cr; 19tl; 24br; 25tc.
N.H.P.A. 38br; /Philippa Scott 39cr; 42bl.
Oxford Scientific Films 35tr; 36cr.
Peale Museum, Baltimore 15cl.
Pennsylvania Academy of Fine Arts 14tr.
Planet Earth /Richard Coomber 39cl; 47cr.
Ann Ronan at Image Select 10bl; 50tl.
Royal Society 19ct; 24tl; 29tl.
St Pauls Girls School 52tl.
Science Museum Photo Library 7tr.
Science Photo Library /Jean Loup
Charmet 16tl; 17bl; 29cl; NASA 29bc;
46cr; 50c; 50cb; 50tr; 52cl; /David Parker
54tl; /Eric Grave 56cl; /Sinclair
Stammers 56cr; Jean Loup Charmet 58tl;
/Novosti 58bl.
Transylvania University Library, Special
Collections, Kentucky 22tl.
Professor H. B. Whittington, University
of Cambridge 46tl; 47tl; 60bl.
Zefa 37cl; 49tr; 56tl.

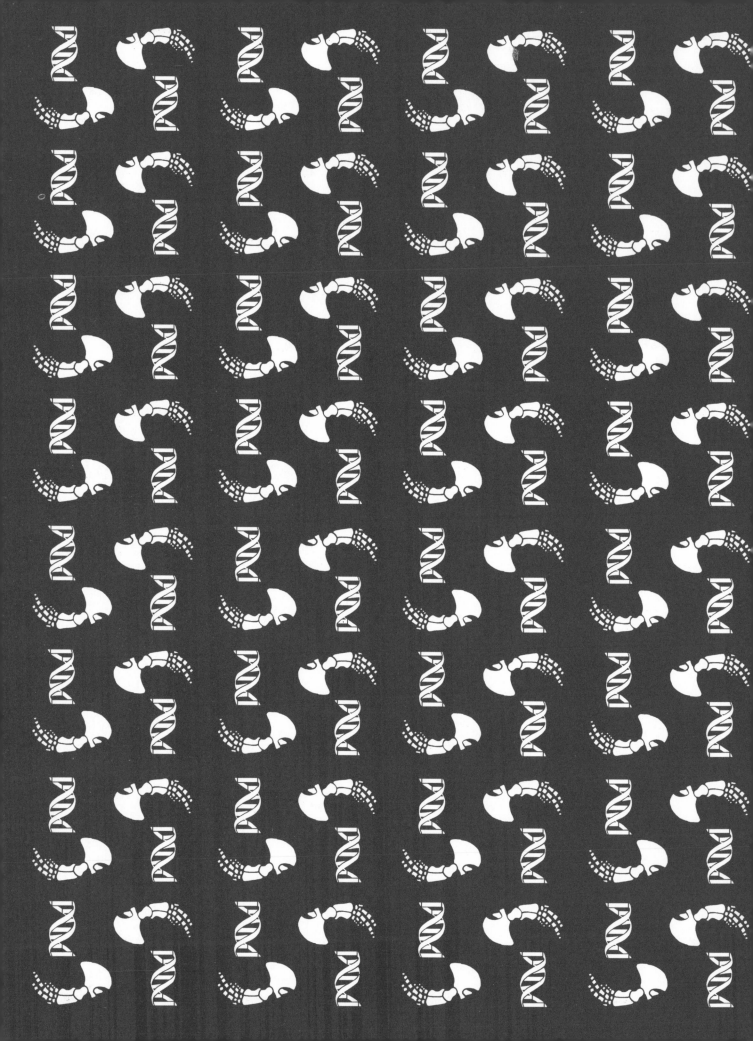